INSIDE THE
PRIMARY SCHOOL

INSIDE THE
PRIMARY SCHOOL

John Blackie

With a Foreword by Lady Plowden

SCHOCKEN BOOKS • NEW YORK

Foreword

by Lady Plowden,
Chairman of the Central Advisory Council for Education
(England) whose report Children and their Primary Schools
was published in January 1967 and is known as the Plowden
Report.

This is a book to be welcomed. It describes for the general reader the primary schools of England today. It tells how the schools and their curriculum developed, how they are organised, and how and what the children in them are learning.

There has been a great wind of change in the primary schools since most of the adults of today were primary school children and many of the old beliefs have been blown away. New and exciting things are happening; this is the only stage in the whole of education when the child is educated as a whole person, and his many interests can be encouraged. Formal examinations are far away, there is no specialisation in subjects and the child can range freely over the wide field of knowledge within his comprehension. There is a greater emphasis on the child learning, rather than on the child being taught. One is an active process while the other may well be passive. We all know that you can take a horse to the water but you cannot make him drink. It has been thought in the past that you could send a child to school and make him learn. The new methods in the primary schools have shown how much more the child learns and how high can be his achievement if instead of being made to learn, the emphasis is on making him want to learn. This is one of the most important skills of the teacher.

There is however an even stronger influence than the school in the education of the child, and this is his home and all that goes on there. If these two powerful influences are kept apart or, which is worse, pull in different directions, the educational development of the child is hampered. His life should not be in separate compartments, with lack of understanding

iii

between home and school. Education is not a thing apart from living, it is part of living itself. Education can only be lived to the full by the child if it is valued and understood by his parents and by the community within which he lives. It is essential therefore that all who are parents and all who have the interests of children at heart should know and care about schools and all that goes on inside them.

John Blackie has given a rounded and lively picture of the schools showing his affection and understanding of the children in them and drawing on the vast knowledge he has acquired about them during a third of a century. He has recently retired from being an H.M.I. As Chief Inspector for Primary Education his wisdom and experience were at the disposal of teachers all over the country. Now his special knowledge makes the schools come alive for a far wider public.

Bridget Plowden

The publishers are grateful to the copyright holders for permission to reproduce the illustrations printed here and to the schools whose work is illustrated.

Bristol City Council

James Galt & Co. Ltd.

Yorkshire (West Riding) County Council

Miss E. E. Biggs

Mrs. D. E. Whittaker

Mr. Alvin Hertzberg

Contents

Introduction

This is a book about primary schools. In this country 'primary school' means any school for children of under 12 years of age. It includes nursery schools for children of 3 and 4, infants' schools for children of 5, 6 and sometimes 7 and junior schools for children of 7 to 11+. These terms, 'nursery', 'infant' and 'junior' have been in use for many years and are those which will be familiar to readers. For that reason I shall use them, but if the recommendations of the Plowden Report* (January 1967) are adopted, the terms 'infant' and 'Junior' will be dropped and we shall talk about 'first' schools and 'middle' schools. In addition, children will stay in the 'first' schools until they are 8 or more and in the 'middle' schools until they are 12½. Middle schools are already being started in some areas and more are being planned.

This book is not written for primary teachers or for people professionally connected with primary education. It is for parents and grandparents, for students in colleges of education, for anyone who, for any reason, wants to know what primary schools are like and why they are like what they are. This is not a history of primary education and most of the book is about the present, but the present cannot be understood without some knowledge of what went before it, so that there are some references to schools as they used to be. Again, this is not a book about the theory of learning but something must be said about the principles which lie behind the various methods and practices described, so there is a chapter called "How children learn". It is not a book about

* See p. 147.

child development but, unless the education of children is in harmony with the way they grow it will not be much good, so there is a chapter called "How children grow".

All the time we shall be thinking about children and about the ways in which parents and teachers can co-operate to help them.

The book was commissioned by the Department of Education and Science, but they have allowed me to write it as a personal account and to express my own views. It was my great good fortune to spend thirty-three years as one of H.M. Inspectors of Schools and it is on this experience, which took me in to primary schools in every part of England, that I have drawn. Although an H.M.I. has the right of entry to any school and classroom in England, I always thought it a privilege to be allowed to see so many teachers and children at work, and I am deeply grateful for the great kindness and forbearance shown to me by the teachers and for all I learned from them and from the children. They gave me a lifetime of interest and happiness and I hope that this book will convey to the general reader something of the excitement of the English primary school at its best.

J.E.H.B.

January 1967.

Note:

The central national authority for Education has had three different names since 1903. The following table of these names, with the titles of the political heads, will help the reader to appreciate the references to them in the text.

1903–1944   Board of Education (President)
1944–1964   Ministry of Education (Minister)
1964–   Department of Education and Science
             (Secretary of State)

Local Education Authorities (referred to in the text as L.E.A.s) are responsible for all maintained schools in England and Wales.

INSIDE THE
PRIMARY SCHOOL

CHAPTER ONE

The old and the new

The old term was 'elementary school'. You see them as you drive through the back streets of great cities, grimy red-brick buildings, surrounded by small areas of asphalt with the W.C.s in detached blocks (because of the smell) or, a little further from the centre, massive 3 or 4-storeyed places with rather larger playgrounds, still all asphalt and still with detached W.C. blocks. In the villages, they are sometimes rather attractive, next door to the church, often with a rather churchy look themselves and with a garden and some trees. But, before they were modernised in the last 20 years or so, these village schools were often as bad in their way as those in the back streets. Some of them still are. They have no hot water, no cloakroom, a tiny box of a room for the infants and some very primitive W.C.s across the playground. Indeed, within living memory, there was a school in a remote area which had no W.C.s. A convenient hedge in an adjoining field, boys on one side, girls on the other, provided all that was thought necessary.

These elementary schools were schools for the poor. We do not talk about the poor now. We call them "the underprivileged" or "the deprived" but we mean the same thing, except that when they were called "the poor" they were a much larger section of the population than they are now, and were relatively much worse off. It is not true that, before 1870 when the power of making elementary education compulsory was granted to the School Boards, that there were no schools for the poor. There were many endowed independent schools where education was free or obtainable for a very small fee. But there were not enough of them and they were not always in the right places. A small market town might have two schools because two rich merchants, one in the 17th century and another in the 18th, had left money for education in their wills, whilst a growing industrial city might have only the one which in the 16th century was quite enough for its needs. Before 1870, if you wanted to be sure of your children's going to school, you had to pay for it out of your own pocket.

The idea of making education available to everybody, whether they could pay for it or not, when it was first suggested was not universally popular. Many of the rich did not like it, partly because they would have to pay for it and partly because they thought that it would put the wrong ideas into the heads of the poor. Dickens' unpleasant Mr. Dombey remarked: "I am far from being friendly to what is called by persons of levelling sentiments, general education. But it is necessary that the inferior classes should continue to be taught to know their position and to conduct themselves properly. So far, I approve of schools." Perhaps it is not quite fair to quote a character in fiction, but there must have been many in 1846, when *Dombey and Son* was published, who thought like that. 'The poor', too, were far from being universally pleased at the prospect of their children's going to school. Many thought education unnecessary, especially for girls, and feared the loss of the money which their children would be prevented from earning if they had to go to school.

When elementary education began to become compulsory in 1870 there already existed large numbers of Church Schools (Anglican, Free Church and Roman Catholic) which had been built at various dates in the previous sixty years by public subscription or, very frequently, at the expense of a single person. To these were now added the so-called Board Schools, administered by the local School Boards, elected bodies set up by the Education Act. These new buildings were very similar to those of the Church Schools. As we look at them now they seem clearly to have been run up "on the cheap" and to have been designed for a very limited education for working-class children who, after a brief exposure to what they had to offer, would know as much as was necessary for the state of life to which they had been called.

This was quite true, but it must be remembered that independent schools, schools for 'the rich', were at that time almost as austere and comfortless, and the curriculum, though different because it included Latin and Greek, as narrow and restricted. Discipline was equally harsh at both kinds of school and thrashings were daily occurrences. The teachers at the best independent schools were better educated than those at the elementary schools and rather better paid, but many of them were grossly inefficient. Altogether there were rather fewer differences between maintained and independent schools in the '70's than might now be supposed. But there was one enormous difference. The elementary schools were for the working class. Anyone who could afford it, sent his children to the independent schools. Not only were there the big Public Schools of ancient origin, Eton, Winchester, Harrow and so on, all of which admitted boys of 8 or 9 or even less, there were also the 19th-century schools, Marlborough, Wellington, Bradfield, Radley, etc. which had been founded to meet the demands of the swelling upper middle class and which also until, about 1870, took boys of primary age. In addition there were large numbers of small, privately-owned concerns, which provided for the children of anyone who considered himself a cut above the working-class and could afford to pay the fees. It must be remembered that the working class at that time were a very rough lot indeed, their children often unshod and in rags and usually unwashed. It was not altogether surprising that those who had been born to a slightly better social position and even more perhaps those who had risen to it, should wish to guard their young from association with the Board School children.

The reader may feel, at this point, that all this is such ancient history that it really has little to do with the schools of today to which his children go or are going. But buildings, teachers and education do not change overnight and even 1870 is not very far away in terms of changing a whole educational system. The writer of this work is 62, an age at which most teachers think of retiring. His father was born in 1867, three years before the first beginnings of compulsory education and his grandfather in 1843, ten years after the first grant of public money to education. When we are considering the schools of 1870 we are not reading about our remote ancestors.

The elementary schools, as they were still called, of the period between the wars (1918–1939), had changed since the end of the 19th century but they had not changed very much. The buildings were the same ones and those which had been put up between, say, 1900 and 1914, were similar to those of 1870. The curriculum had expanded but the emphasis was still on the 3 Rs. Some of the teachers were better educated and trained, but there were still large numbers of untrained teachers (unqualified) and, in charge of infants' classes, many 'supplementaries' who needed only to be British and vaccinated. The children were still mainly working-class, and it was still almost unheard of for any members of the professional classes, apart from teachers, to send their children to the elementary schools.

In 1924 something happened which was destined to change the whole face of English education. The President of the Board of Education (now called The Secretary of State for Education) referred to a consultative committee under the chairmanship of Sir Henry Hadow the whole range of elementary education. This committee wrote three reports— *The Education of the Adolescent* (1927), *The Primary School* (1931) and *Infant and Nursery Schools* (1934). It is sometimes said that the appointment of a committee and the issue of a report is the best way of looking as if you are doing something without actually doing it. This was certainly not true of the Hadow Committee. Their most far-reaching recommendation was that the old elementary school, which had had an age-range of 5 to 14, should be split in two. The younger part, with children of 5 to 11, should be called the Primary School and the older part, 11 to 14, the Senior Elementary School. This re-organisation which had already taken place here and there by L.E.A. initiative, gathered speed after 1927 and by 1939 had affected about one-third of the children in England. Children who could pass the entrance examination and whose parents wished them to go had for long left the elementary schools at the age of 11 and had gone on to the

Grammar Schools, leaving the rest to complete their education where they had begun it. Now, however, all children were to have a change of school at 11. Those who could manage it went, as before, to the Grammar School and the rest to the Senior School. These Senior Schools were the forerunners of the Secondary Modern Schools which were established in 1945.

This is a book about primary schools and it is not necessary to pursue the story of the older children beyond this point. The primary schools did not, of course, come into existence simultaneously. The Hadow re-organisation was patchy and in 1939, as we have seen, only complete in a minority of areas. Indeed it was only completed all over the country in 1965. The first primary schools began as remnants. They were what was left when the older children were taken away to the Senior Schools. It was not till just before the war, and then only in a few areas, that new primary schools were established. The word used in the early 1930s was 'decapitation', and many head teachers felt just like that. The older children, of whom they were very proud and whom many of them had taught almost exclusively, had gone, and they were 'left with the kids'. It must be remembered that, at that time, there was nothing like the anxiety to get to a Grammar School that there was later on. The parents of many children who had passed the examination (the 11+ as it came to be called) did not take up the offered places. In any elementary school, therefore, the top class (Standard 7 or sometimes X-7) was likely to contain a number of very clever children whom it had been the head teacher's special joy to teach. It was hardly to be wondered at if the early primary schools suffered from depression.

The depression was much more evident in the junior schools than in the Infants' Schools. In the country, and in small schools generally, primary schools were single schools under one head teacher, but wherever the schools were larger, they were divided into two departments, juniors and infants, each with its own head teacher. The United Kingdom, Israel and New Zealand are alone in beginning compulsory education at 5.[1] In most countries, including the U.S.A. and the U.S.S.R. it begins at 6 or 7. The English Infants'

School, therefore, developed on its own lines and it was here that most of the new educational ideas which have now spread upwards into the junior schools, were first tried out. What these ideas were and what they have done and are doing to primary schools today we shall consider in a moment. Before doing so let us have a look at a typical primary school just before the war.

The building is almost certainly old. Most of the new buildings of the 1930s were for senior schools and only on new estates were young children taught in up-to-date buildings. In a large city school there would probably be a hall, with classrooms opening off it and, as often as not, the head teacher's desk would be in the hall so that he or she might keep an eye on all that went on. In smaller schools, whether in town or country, there might be no hall and some-times no room for the head teacher, who would sit in the classroom in which he taught. The children would spend much of the day sitting at double desks or sometimes long desks without backs, and they would either be receiving instruction in the form of class-lessons or be performing tasks of writing, reading or learning by heart. They would seldom, often never, have any opportunity of choosing what they did. Set exercises, set compositions, set books, set drawings or paintings, set music, set physical exercises, set lessons— these dominated most of the day in most schools. Many teachers showed great skill in handling large classes and in getting the children to work. The best teachers managed to infuse a remarkable amount of interest into this very rigid framework and a few were beginning to break away from it and encourage more initiative and enterprise in the children.

At 8.55 a.m. the bell would ring and the children line up in the playground. They would be marched in by their teachers while the piano in the hall played Colonel Bogey or the March in Scipio, and would take their places for Assembly, which consisted of a prayer or two and some hymns. They would then march out to their classrooms, where they would receive half-an-hour's religious instruction before turning, throughout the school, to Arithmetic which would last till break. After break would come English in various forms. At intervals during the morning the rhythm would be broken and a class would go into the playground (or the hall, if there was one, if it was wet) for what was still quite often called 'drill'. For this the children wore their ordinary clothes and shoes. They stood in lines, boys at the front, girls at the back, so that in bending exercises the girls should not show their underclothes to the boys, and did exercises, of the kind known in the Army as physical jerks.

In 1933 the Board of Education published a new Physical Training Syllabus which involved a lot more free movement and such things as handstands, skipping, jumping, balancing and so on. This meant that special shoes and clothing were almost indispensable. But there was no money to buy either and, if the parents could not or would not supply their children with gym shoes, they had to continue to wear heavy day shoes or even clogs. And special clothing was even more difficult. Boys showed great reluctance to remove even their jackets and pullovers, let alone their shirts and vests, and it was not uncommon to find a class of girls standing on their heads, their skirts inside out round their chests, because this exercise was prescribed 'by the Board', but to take off one's skirt was indecent! At one school, where the parents had objected strongly to any removal of clothing for P.T. a single demonstration on an open day was enough to convince them that their attitude served neither decency nor free movement.

P.E. then was one of the breakthroughs and by 1939 the lessons were much freer and more informal and it was increasingly rare to find the children unsuitably clothed. The boys' mothers had discovered that their sons did not die of pneumonia if they shed anyhow some outer layers, and the girls, from school funds or parental contribution, usually wore dark blue shorts or knickers which allowed uninhibited movement. Another breakthrough was in Art. Instead of being told to draw, with a hard HB. pencil on white paper, a daffodil or a hockey-stick, or to make a geometrical pattern and colour it red and yellow, the children began to be allowed to paint their own pictures, with large brushes, plentiful powder-paint and large pieces of kitchen-paper. This change was due chiefly to Marion Richardson of the

L.C.C. and her name should be remembered with gratitude. It showed that children seemed to know almost instinctively what to do with paint, just as they had always known what to do with water and sand. They set about making pictures with great concentration and purpose and the pictures they made were vivid and exciting.

If P.E. and Art showed the first signs of a general loosening-up in schools there were, as the decade went on, increasing though still very small numbers of schools which were carrying the same sort of ideas into other parts of the curriculum. I remember a headmaster saying to me in 1938: "If these children have so much to say and say it so well in pictorial art, why should we not give them the same freedom in written English?" He did not get further than asking the question, and another headmaster, a few streets away, to whom I had suggested the institution of *one hour a week* during which the children should choose their occupation, replied that this was impossible because they would not know what to do. The log-jam was breaking up very slowly.

It is worth while stopping for a moment to consider why this was so. After all, the ideas which were opposed to a rigid formal education for young children had been current for a long time. As long ago as 1826 Froebel had said that play was the foundation of learning and in 1875 the Froebel Society was founded to propagate his principles in the United Kingdom. Since then other educational thinkers had continued on the same lines and numbers of independent schools had been established to put them into practice. Why were the Public Elementary Schools so slow in trying them out? It would be wrong to blame the teachers. As we have seen, many were untrained and had received a very limited secondary education. Many of the training colleges had a very restricted and restrictive view of their job and some were surprisingly out of touch with modern thought. The teachers had, as they still have, a deep sense of responsibility to their children. They did not wish to subject them to experiments which might be harmful. They knew the importance to many of them of success in examinations, and this seemed to them more likely to follow from traditional methods than from experimental ones. Added to this it must be admitted that it is always easier to continue on familiar lines, particularly when not very much is done to help you to explore the new ones. Until 1898 teachers had had to teach what they were told and their salaries had depended partly on their children's performance in an annual examination conducted by H.M. Inspectors. There were no teachers at work in the 1930s who had had first-hand experience of those times but the senior ones had grown up with older colleagues who had, and the fear of the inspector took a long time to die.

How then did the changes come about, if there were so many influences which were hostile to change? Firstly, however gingerly some teachers grasped it, the freedom of the individual head teacher was genuine. He* had a far wider latitude in deciding what to teach, how to teach it and what books to use than was or is enjoyed by the head teachers in any other country in the world. Secondly, the influences at work on him were becoming more experimental in outlook. The training colleges rather slowly, H.M. Inspectorate more quickly, became the agents of innovation. In-service training courses which before 1914 had not existed and in the 1920s had been rare, began to increase. The Hadow report on *The Primary School* (1931) was beginning to be read and it gave respectability to ideas which had hitherto been thought of as cranky or idealistic. Nevertheless, at the outbreak of the war, the number of junior schools which had been substantially affected was very small and even in the infants' schools, which had started earlier and moved faster, there was still a solid block of conservatism.

The war was a disaster for education as for every other liberal growth, but it was not an unmitigated disaster.

---

* I have, with much reluctance, decided to use 'he', 'him' and 'his' when writing of teachers, except when the reference is specifically to nursery or infants' schools where nearly all the teachers are women. To have used the feminine pronouns and adjectives throughout would have been to give the impression that practically all primary teachers are women. Twenty years ago this would have been true but more and more men are taking up primary teaching and I thought that the legal convention (for purposes of this Act 'man' includes 'woman') was the best one to adopt.

Evacuation and bombing broke up the schools but they forced all teachers into a new relationship with the children, jerked everybody out of their ruts and made all sorts of improvisations and makeshifts necessary. Teachers who had taught the same stuff in the same city classroom for fifteen years found themselves in the fens, or the hills, or the farmlands, the only link with the children's background, and they simply had to re-think what they were doing. More generally the war caused widespread questioning and in 1945 the climate was favourable to change. The need to increase the teaching force rapidly led to the establishment of Emergency Training Colleges for Teachers.[2] Into these came, for a year's intensive course, young men, not straight from school, but who had, a few months before, been fighter pilots, commandos, submarine crew and so on, and who, a year later, brought into the schools a very different outlook on life from that of those who had formed the staffs in the 1930s. The situation was more fluid than it had ever been before.

Even so the changes did not come with a rush. Some of the old brakes still operated and one had appeared which, if not new, was now much more formidable than it had been before the war—the 11+ examination. Until 1944 (the Butler Act) most Grammar Schools had had a proportion of fee-paying children. The standard of admission for them was supposed to be the same as for the free-place or 'scholarship' children, but in fact most grammar schools had some discretion in the matter and admitted fee-payers who showed promise and whose parents seemed likely to help them with an intelligent interest in their education, even if their marks were not up to standard. Thus it was that only rarely did the child of well-to-do middle-class parents fail to gain a grammar school place, whilst the child of working-class parents who could not afford the fees could only gain admission if he scored enough marks. This was not quite as unfair as it now sounds. The working class, as we have seen, often did not accept places when they were offered and, though this was unfair to the children, it was not the direct result of the method of admission. Further, as we now know, the single most important factor in success at school is parental interest, and the existence of this was really quite a good reason for selecting a child for a grammar school education. Nevertheless the system was not really defensible and in 1944 all fee-paying places were abolished. A child whose parents wanted him to go to a grammar school had now either to pass the 11+ or be sent to an independent school which, if it was any good, would charge much higher fees than his father would have had to pay under the old arrangement at a grammar school. The effect of the 1944 decision was a boom in independent schools and an enormously increased pressure for success in the 11+, a pressure in which the working class now joined. In all areas, but particularly in those favoured by the middle class, schools were made aware of parental anxiety and some, in which the head teacher was trying to introduce experimental methods, were subjected to strong parental complaints. The effect on the children was of course bad. Some were offered bribes in the shape of bicycles or model railways, so that to failure in the examination was added the failure to acquire a much longed-for possession. There was no end to the follies committed. To read the correspondence columns of the press at that time (1947–1953 or thereabouts) you would have supposed that the teachers of England had gone mad, that they had thrown to the winds, discipline, accuracy, care and hard work and were inflicting upon the children untried, wild-cat things called 'activity methods'. In this they were being aided and abetted, it was said, by H.M. Inspectors. This story, quite literally, got abroad, and the Ministry (now the Department) was constantly being asked by foreign visitors to be shown 'activity schools'. The request was referred to H.M.I.s who found great difficulty in discovering any! Change was taking place, but much more slowly and cautiously and sensibly than the agonised voices of the critics suggested. It is the object of this book to describe those changes and the state of primary schools today.

There are about 23,000 primary schools in England and Wales, in which some 150,000 teachers teach. No system of such a size, however hard everyone tried to make it so, could be uniformly excellent or anything else. In the Plowden

Report (January 1967) an account is given of a study made by
H.M. Inspectors in 1964.[3] This showed that something like a
third of the schools have been substantially affected by
change in outlook and method, another third somewhat
affected and the remaining third very little affected. This
is what might be expected. If it is stated in the form of a
graph it is represented by a beehive-shaped curve. This
does not mean that the schools in the bottom third of the
curve are without merit, or that the children are necessarily
unhappy in them. They may have solid virtues and the
teachers may have the children's welfare at heart. It simply
means that they approach their work more on the lines of the
1930s than do the schools in the top third. These are all
trying to teach the children according to modern ideas.
Some of them are doing it supremely well. It is of these
latter that I shall principally be thinking as I write, because
it is these schools which are most interesting and, I imagine,
most in need of being described and explained to the
ordinary reader. The Plowden Council, after spending three
years in a minute examination of primary schools, came out,
on the whole, as supporters of the modern approach and it is
reasonable to expect that the primary school of the future
will move broadly in that direction.

As we mentioned earlier, the number of new primary
schools built between the wars was not very great. Between
1919 and 1944 2,483 such schools housing 675 thousand
children were built. Since 1945 we have done rather better.
Nearly 5,000 primary schools housing 1,200,000 children
have been built, which means that getting on for a quarter of
the primary schools in England have been put up since the
end of the second war. But there is still a long way to go. In
1962 there were 6,580 primary schools in use which had
been built before 1875 and another 5,986 built before 1902.[4]

The new buildings which were put up in the years
immediately following the war were still essentially similar to
those of the 1930s. They were lighter and more attractive
but they still consisted of a number of rectangular classrooms, a hall, offices, passageways and playground. In recent
years, however, the changes which this book describes have

influenced school design and a very different sort of primary school building has begun to appear. It is worth mentioning that the new buildings cost substantially less than the old ones but are much better adapted to the needs of primary education as they now appear. The latest of these schools, the Eveline Lowe School, Rolls Road, London S.E.1, may be taken as an example. The following description of it is adapted from the Plowden Report (Vol. 1, p. 400).

This school was designed by the Department's Development Group in collaboration with the Inner London Education Authority within the current cost limit. (This is £340 a place compared with £200 in 1949.) The accommodation was planned for the following groupings of the 320 pupils:

Two nursery groups of 30 children.

Four "family" groups of 40 children with an age-range of about two years.

Two groups of older children, one of 40 and one of 60, to be looked after by more than one teacher.

The architects fitted their design to educational requirements and the main features which emerged from this were:

  i. The sub-division of the available space to allow small groups of children to pursue widely varying activities.

  ii. A difference in character, i.e. finish, scale, colour, lighting, furniture, floor-coverings, between small, quiet areas, general working areas and areas equipped for the messier kinds of work. The quiet areas are carpeted.

  iii. Direct access at many points to sheltered verandahs and the ground outside.

The whole school, inside and outside was conceived as potential teaching space. There is no hard and fast division between the group spaces mentioned above and the rest of the school, no closed classrooms, shut off from each other and from the passages and playgrounds.

A building like this only makes sense if the teaching and learning that go on in it are different from the traditional kind with which most readers are familiar. What is described in the later chapters of this book can and does go on in the old school buildings, including many in which there are great handicaps for the teachers and children to overcome. The new kind of building makes the new approach easier and the old one more difficult. To that extent it forces the teachers hands. When one such building was opened the head teacher and her assistant who had been appointed to take charge of it had hitherto been pretty traditional in their methods, but they soon found that the new building opened up all sorts of possibilities, both to them and to the children, which they had hardly dreamed of before they moved in. The building took charge, but there is no question of this process becoming a stampede. The supply of old buildings will last for many years and there will be a long time for experiment before they are completely replaced.

CHAPTER TWO

How children grow

Whatever a school provides in the way of discipline, teaching, books and apparatus will only be useful if it 'fits' the children. We should all agree that the schools described in Dickens' novels—Mr. Creakle's school in *David Copperfield*, Dotheboy's Hall in *Nicholas Nickleby*, the school in *Hard Times* and the school conducted by Mr. Wopsle's great aunt in *Great Expectations*—were dreadful, and that they failed completely to provide for the nature and needs of children. Such extreme examples are easy to recognise. But is enough known about how children grow and how they learn to be sure about how they ought to be brought up and taught?

In the last chapter we saw that many schools had changed since the war and were still changing, some faster than others, some a great deal, some hardly at all. These changes have been made because teachers believed that they fitted what was known about children better than the traditional ways. If *all* the facts about children's growth and ways of learning were known perhaps all schools would be more alike, but there is still much that is not known. It would not be sensible to let everything remain unchanged until all the facts are known. That, in any case, is unlikely ever to happen. All that teachers can do is to found their practice on a combination of their own experience and intuition, and the knowledge about growth and development and learning which research has made available. If they rely too much on the former they will certainly miss the advantages that knowledge gives and they may allow principles to harden into prejudices and insight to be obscured by dogma. If, on the other hand, they follow too slavishly the direction of research, their contact with the children is blunted and they become transmitters instead of dynamos. Only the combination will really do.

About the physical growth of children in general much is known. It is known that they grow very rapidly in their first year, that their growth rate decreases quite steadily until puberty is reached, that from about the age of six until puberty the rate of decrease is nearly constant and that at puberty a spurt begins and that, for two years or so, they grow at about the same rate as when they were two or three. This is a perfectly true general statement and were it precisely true of every individual child the teacher's lot might be easier. There are, however, differences between the growth of boys and girls, and quite big differences between individuals. The growth differences between boys and girls are not either very great or, from the teacher's point of view, very important in the early years, but girls begin their adolescent spurt, on the average, two years earlier than boys. This makes for certain difficulties at the top of the primary school and will make for even more if the age of transfer is raised to 12 or 13. First of all it means that from about 11 to 14 girls are taller, heavier and often stronger than boys. But boys expect to be taller, heavier and stronger than girls, which a little later on they *will* be and, in a co-educational school (and nearly all primary schools *are* co-educational) they may make constant efforts to behave as if they were. Secondly, it means that some of the girls at the top of the primary school will be physically women. This is more of a problem now than it was before the war, because the age at which girls begin to menstruate is becoming gradually earlier, at a rate of about 4 months in every decade. This is happening all over the world, for reasons that are by no means clear. Obviously it will stop somewhere and might even go into reverse, but it has greatly increased the number of pubescent girls in the primary school and will increase it even more if the age is raised. This means that the children who take the lead— the seniors—in the primary school will consist of two inharmonious groups—girls who have already begun to acquire the feelings and instincts of women and boys who remain little boys.

Differences between individual children of the same sex

are in some ways even more troublesome. Not only all laws
and regulations but also the expectations of parents and of
children themselves are based on chronological age. School
attendance begins at 5. Parents tell their children: 'Now you
are 8 you must behave like a big boy'. Elder sisters will say:
'Fancy still playing with dolls when you are 13!' and children
of 6 will feel a sense of superiority over those who are 'only
5'. All this is built on something which is practically meaningless. Chronological age is convenient only because it is
exactly known. It tells you little that is important about a
child and conceals much that is vital.

The time at which the misleading nature of chronological
age can be most clearly seen is at puberty. Menstruation in
girls begins, on average, at 13.[5] The normal range, for 95%
of girls, is from 10 to 15, but the extreme range (99% of
girls) is from 9 to 16. A class of 11–12 year old girls will thus
contain some in whom puberty has not yet started, some who
are fully developed and possibly even a few who are capable
of bearing children. With boys the age of greatest variation
comes later (13–14) but the physical differences are even
more dramatic.

These physical differences cause quite enough difficulties
in themselves. A 14-year-old boy whose puberty has not yet
begun may feel desperately worried about it. He cannot
compete in height or strength with his contemporaries and
his hairless body and undeveloped genitals may seem to be a
continual reproach to him. The 13-year-old girl whose chest
is still flat and who is still bored by the talk about boys that
goes on among her more developed companions may feel
terribly out of it. Time will put the matter right but the
agony can be very hard to bear while it lasts. For this variation in the rate of physical development is also characteristic of emotional and intellectual development. To talk
about 'what a child ought to know' when he is 11, or 12 or 13
is to talk nonsense. It only makes sense if the reference is to
developmental not chronological age.

This makes for a whole crop of difficulties. It would be
convenient if we could find some reliable way of measuring
developmental age so that there would be information about

each child as simple and as indisputable as his chronological age and yet corresponding to something relevant. The development of the bone structure of his body can be measured with great accuracy by means of X-rays of the wrist. These bones undergo a sequence of changes from birth onwards which is practically the same in everybody, while the age at which any particular stage is reached varies considerably, both as between boys and girls and as between individuals. If this bone-age corresponded to emotional, sexual, 'motor' skill and intellectual stages of development, it would provide a most convenient general factor. Unfortunately, although it does constitute a pretty reliable predictor of the age at which full adult height will be reached and at which menstruation will begin, it is not closely related to the growth of intelligence or motor skill.

The situation is thus, that, for administrative purposes, we are obliged to fall back on the convenient but thoroughly misleading chronological age. Parents and teachers must realise how meaningless this is and, even more difficult, try to help children to accept and live with wide differences in stages of development. During the long journey from birth to maturity it is probable that there are a number of critical periods. This is certainly so in many of the lower animals. If a certain stimulus is withheld during one of these periods, the response to it never develops in later life however strongly the stimulus is applied. Whether this is so in the development of children is less certain, but there is little doubt that they have certain strong needs at particular stages and that, if these needs are denied, their development suffers. For instance, babies need cuddling. They need the constant feel of their mother's bodies and the physical expressions of her love and care. That is beyond question. There is some reason to think that, if they are not given this and affection is withheld from them, their power to give and to respond to affection later on is gravely impaired. The adolescent delinquent, callous and indifferent to the feelings of others, may be the uncuddled baby of 15 years earlier.

We must now consider how much of all this development is dependent on heredity and how much on upbringing, or to use more scientific terms, how much is genetic in origin and how much environmental. Not very long ago attempts were made to express these two influences as percentages. It would be said that 60% of a person's characteristics were genetic and 40% environmental. The old proverb 'you can't make a silk purse out of a sow's ear' embodied the belief that there are innate qualities and abilities which nothing can alter. For a long time intelligence testing and the use of Intelligence Quotients reinforced this belief. On the other hand, Marxist thinkers repudiated the notion and seemed to believe that environment was responsible for everything and that, if there *were* innate differences, education, in its early stages at least, should take no account of them.

It is always unfortunate when essentially educational matters get mixed up with politics, though of course politics is inevitably and properly concerned with education. Insistence on inherited abilities sometimes aroused the suspicion that this was a disguised way of preserving a class structure, and it was doubtless this which produced the extreme egalitarianism of the Marxist. In England we have had an educational system which assumed that there were great differences between children and attempted to provide for them. Streaming and selection at 11+ were two devices for achieving this. We are now moving against selection and, rather less resolutely, against streaming, but both of them are still controversial issues.

It is therefore important to understand as far as we can, what is really known about heredity and environment. Unfortunately it is not possible to explain this in very simple words, and without the use of scientific terms. The reader must bear with me if he finds the next page or two rather heavy going.

It is clear that heredity and environmental factors are both important. No theory which tries to ignore or play down either has any validity. The development of every person is the result of interaction between these two sets of factors *and* between the factors in each set. Thus genes are inherited. Immediately the ovum is fertilised in the mother's womb, they begin to act on each other and as the foetus grows, the

interaction between its various parts becomes more complex. The environment at this stage is the mother's body. It
is thus true that no characteristics are inherited. All of them
are developed as a consequence of interaction. But no
characteristic *can* develop unless it has the necessary genetic
endowment to provide a basis for development. The genetic
endowment of each individual is final and unalterable.

We may take height as a fairly simple and uncontroversial
example of a characteristic. Why are some people taller than
others? The answer varies in different parts of the world,
though it is everywhere true that the variation is partly
attributable to genetic factors. In England, where most
children have enough to eat, i.e. when the environment is
favourable to physical growth, the variation is mainly due to
inheritance. But in countries where the environment is
unfavourable, where children are undernourished and thus
more prone to disease, more of the variation will be due to
environment. Moreover, the responses made to the environment by individuals will be partly genetic and thus will not be
identical. If two undernourished children are given the same
amount of extra nutrition they will not necessarily grow
correspondingly in height. In other words an environment
may be favourable to a child with certain genes and less
favourable or even unfavourable to a child with different
genes.

It seems likely, though in this matter it is far less easy to be
certain, that all that has been said about the characteristic of
height is equally true of the characteristic of intelligence.
But, while height is exactly measurable and beyond argument, intelligence is much less easily measurable and far
more open to dispute. It is not even exactly definable or at
any rate, not everyone will agree with any particular definition that we may adopt. However we all know pretty well
what we mean by it and would perhaps assent to a definition
by Sir Cyril Burt.[6] He calls it 'innate, general, cognitive
efficiency'. Innate, because however possible it be to improve
and develop it, it is basically a genetic endowment, general
because it can be applied over a wide field of activity and not
just a single one, and cognitive because it involves knowing.

So far as parents are concerned the controversy begins when we come to the various means devised for testing it.

This chapter is about how children grow and it is not the place for a full description and discussion of intelligence testing. Parents, however, will want to know at least whether the tests are reliable and whether they are final, i.e. whether if a child's I.Q. is 90 at 8, it will go on being 90 for the rest of his life. There are some other questions too which need answering at this point.

First it must be said that, if a test has been properly standardised, that is tried out on sufficient numbers of children chosen at random, it is reliable. But because, in such a sample, there will be a great many children clustered about the mean, i.e. average children, and fewer children at the extremes, i.e. sub-normal and highly gifted children, it follows that the standardisation will be better, and the test therefore more accurate, for the average than for the others. What this means in effect is that two children who 'score' I.Qs of 145 and 150 in the test are both unquestionably very intelligent but the difference between them may not be what their I.Qs suggest. On another test or on the same test another day, the score might be reversed.

At the other end of the scale, a child who scores 75, is, almost beyond doubt, of very low intelligence, but of course if those who know him, his parents and teachers, think that this is not so, the matter should always be investigated. Poor eyesight, or illness or emotional upset could all have caused havoc at the time of the test.

It was at one time believed that intelligence tests tested the innate, genetic factors and that, since these could not be altered, the I.Q. was something constant. The account just given of what is now known about the development of characteristics shows that this belief is no longer tenable. This has led some people to say that intelligence tests are useless and the I.Q. a delusion, but this is going much too far the other way. The I.Q. is not either a perfect selector or an infallible predictor but nor is anything else, and both attainment tests and teachers' reports are at least as likely to be inaccurate and probably rather more so. Intelligence tests are very useful when they are combined with other tests. They provide a check and, if properly designed and administered, they are rather less likely than any other form of test to favour the child from the 'good home'.

It is time to think a little about 'good' homes and 'bad' homes and what home can do to help children to grow fully or to hinder them from doing so. Although this is a book about schools, the home is the place where development begins and at all stages of education it remains the most important influence in a child's life. A home which gives to children protection, warmth, clothing, comfort, cleanliness, food and drink does much to ensure healthy physical growth. Other things being equal, such children will be healthier, better, heavier and stronger than those from homes in which those elements are deficient. But they are not enough to guarantee growth. Shortly after the British forces arrived in Germany in 1945 two children's homes came under the control of the medical services. Both were ordered the rations necessary to restore and maintain their physical well-being. One of the two however was ordered special extra rations in order that the effect of them might be studied and compared with that of the normal rations. To everybody's dismay and bewilderment the children on ordinary rations began to go ahead and those on the extra rations to fall behind. Investigation revealed that by pure coincidence, a nurse had been transferred from the control home to the experimental home at the moment when the experiment started. This woman was particularly disagreeable, harsh and repressive and her transfer was enough to nullify completely the effects of the extra food.[7] The lesson is obvious. I can think of two families that I know, which make the point well. One is rather ramshackle and untidy. Their house is messy and in a poor state of decoration and repair and the children are not always too clean, yet they are happy and they do well at school, because they are loved. The others have a 'House and Garden' home, redecorated annually, with a garden in apple-pie order. The children are spotless. They are not unloved, but the home is designed for the parents and not for them. They must never make a mess and never be dirty.

It was not surprising that before one of them was five she had to go to a psychiatrist. Once again, of course, we are looking at extremes. It is not necessary to be dirty to be happy, and a clean and beautiful home may be a good one for children, but they do need a home in which they can behave as children, and one in which they are loved. If the love is too protective, or too possessive or too conditional on their good behaviour, or capricious, they will suffer.

A great deal has been made recently of the disadvantages suffered by working-class children as compared with middle-class ones. It has been said that the equality of opportunity of which we boast is a fake, because the working-class child starts with a built-in handicap. Obviously there is something in this. If you grow up in a home in which you hear intelligent discussion and conversation, in which there are plenty of good books which you see your parents read, in short with a rich cultural background, you start with an advantage over another child who may be just as intelligent as you are but in whose home there is little conversation, few or no books and generally an impoverished cultural life. If the former kind of home is more characteristic of the middle class and the latter of the working class (and this is a very broad and uncertain distinction) then the conclusion sticks. Recent research, however, seems to suggest, though not to prove, that father's income and occupation, poor housing, and drab surroundings are far less important for a child's success at school than the interest shown by both parents in his work and progress.[8] If further research confirms this, increasing emphasis will have to be placed on the education of parents and perhaps a little less on the importance of socio-economic classes.

Where does all this get us to? We have seen that individual children grow at different speeds, that, though the stages of growth are the same for all, the age at which they are reached varies widely, and that the differences between them are the product of a very complex interaction, which begins at conception, between heredity and environment. It follows from this that we need the most flexible educational system that we can manage. All neat and tidy classifications are wrong.

Age of entry, age of transfer, age of leaving, all expectations
based on chronological age, classification by I.Q. or by
examination, basic curricula, agreed syllabuses and all the
rest are uneducational because they are based on an entirely
obsolete view of growth. That does not mean that we can or
ought to scrap the lot. If every child could have his own
individual teacher that might be possible, but children must,
for much of the time, be taught in groups and this is certainly
a good thing in itself. The system has got to work and it
would be very foolish to scrap the machine before we have
built another. What we are now doing *is* building another.
The changes that have been outlined in Chapter One and
which will be described in more detail in later chapters are
being made because they seem to fit what we now know
about children's growth and learning. They are not changes
for the sake of change, and because we do not know everything we shall make some mistakes. But we do know enough
to go cautiously ahead on this new road.

CHAPTER THREE

How children learn

A reader of this book who had learned, say, bricklaying would probably give some such account as follows of how he'd done it. He would admit first to a motive. There was something—a desire to earn his living as a bricklayer or to be able to build his own garage—which was strong enough to make him decide to learn the craft. This he did by listening to instruction, by watching an expert at work, by 'trying his own hand', by practice and by experience, until he became an expert himself. Another who had learned Italian, after he had left school, would also admit first to a motive which, again, might be very different in different individuals, and to a rather similar process of listening, imitation, practice and experience.

The process of learning has gone on since man first existed and his ideas about it have been expressed in proverbial form. 'You can take a horse to the water but you can't make him drink' is a proverbial way of saying that you must have a motive for learning. 'If at first you don't succeed, try, try, try again' is a recognition that some quality of persistence is needed. 'Practice makes perfect' speaks for itself; 'All work and no play makes Jack a dull boy', in its modern version would be interpreted as meaning that there must be pleasure and delight involved in learning, and 'You must learn to walk before you can run' recognises that there are stages in learning which must be taken in the right order if success is to be achieved.

The human race learned and achieved an enormous amount before anyone ever gave any thought to the learning process, and the individuals that we imagined at the beginning of this chapter learned what they wanted to know without worrying very much about how they did it. Some might feel inclined to say that concern with the theory of learning is waste of time, and that teachers soon discover what methods are effective and then simply build on experience and rely on intuition.

It must be admitted that knowledge of the latest views on the theory of learning is no guarantee by itself of being a good teacher. It must also be admitted that, in young children, the urge to learn is so powerful that they will survive quite a lot of mismanagement and discouragement, though by no means unscathed. And it must be admitted that educational thinkers are not all of one mind about the learning process and that there is a great deal that is still not known about it. These might be read as arguments for leaving the matter to the researchers until they can tell us more, while parents and teachers continue to work intuitively and pragmatically. But there is a rather strong argument against taking such a view.

No one really believes that all children make the most of themselves. It is certain that many children do not learn as much as their parents and teachers hoped, that school is not equally successful with all. In the previous chapter we saw some of the reasons for this. Another one almost certainly is that not enough is known about the needs of children in the process of learning, and that the wrong treatment is given to some of them in school. If we can discover anything about this process which will help us to help children to learn more and to learn better and more easily, we should be very wrong to neglect to do so simply because we cannot discover everything. Basic, scientifically-conducted research is essential, but it needs to be fed by the observation and the trials and errors of countless teachers and parents, which themselves provide part of the material the researchers need. Intuition and experience have not found all the answers, for all the children, all of the time, but it would be a bad day for education if they came into disrepute. The only sensible course is to pursue all the lines of enquiry that look promising. In the account that follows I shall try to show how theory and practice interlock and how the former has influenced the latter in the English primary school of today.

The theory of learning which has received the most general acceptance in England is that propounded by Jean Piaget of Geneva. Piaget and his chief assistant Barbel Inhelder have conducted an immense number of investigations into the ways in which children learn. Piaget began many years ago, with his own children and he has published a formidable body of evidence and theory since. The best summary of Piaget's findings and views is J. M. Hunt's *Intelligence and Experience*. This volume runs to over 400 octavo pages. To attempt a summary in such a book as this would be absurd, but it is possible to describe the basic theory quite briefly, and I think this may be worth doing because the relation between the theory and the best primary school practice is reasonably clear even when the theory is briefly and baldly stated.

Piaget describes learning as being composed of two processes, assimilation and accommodation. Assimilation is what is done to what has to be learned in order that it can be learned, and accommodation is what the learner has to do, as it were, within himself in order to learn. A very simple example may make this clearer. In order to learn to open a door a child has to manipulate the handle, find out whether the door needs pushing or pulling and what the weight of the door is. This is the process of Assimilation. But he must also do the right things, turn the handle the right way, push or pull with appropriate force and thus accommodate himself to the experience of door opening. There is thus established a pattern of behaviour that Piaget calls a *schema* (pl. *schemata*) which is something that can be repeated and generalised. Each time the door is met with the *schema* is repeated. But not all doors are the same. There are different kinds of handles. Some doors have latches. Some open out, some inward. Some are heavy, some are light. These unfamiliar features will each require assimilation and accommodation. The original simple *schema* will have to be modified. Modifications will always be needed whenever a new experience is encountered. An elderly man who thinks he knows all about opening doors will have to assimilate and to accommodate when he first meets one which opens 'by itself', i.e. by a photoelectric cell, as he approaches it. His experience will be momentarily disconcerting, and with a glass door which looks as if it were not there it may even be painful.

The process of assimilation and accommodation begins at birth, increases in intensity in early childhood and continues throughout life, though the ability to assimilate and accommodate in most people declines as they grow older ('you can't teach an old dog new tricks'). The *schemata* (the generalisable and repeatable patterns of behaviour) increase in number, grow more and more complex and interact between each other. In the early stages learning is in the sensori-motor field. That is to say that children must see, hear, feel, smell or taste things in order to learn what they are. They cannot learn by being told. They cannot form abstract or imaginary concepts. They learn too by their own movement. They find that they cannot touch everything that they see. They must stretch out or crawl in order to reach the desired object. Only later can they judge a distance, and, much later on still, understand what is meant when they are told of a distance ('It is five miles from here'). As they grow older the pattern of behaviour begins to include patterns of thought. They can assimilate abstractions and accommodate themselves to them. A new theorem, a new mathematical process, a discussion of a 17th-century political issue, a debate on the existence of God—the process remains essentially the same. But by the time that this stage of learning is reached the individual has undergone an immensely complex transformation. Each new experience, however slight, has had to be assimilated and the resultant accommodation has slightly modified the whole system of *schemata* which add up to the individual as he is. No one perhaps ever stops learning altogether, but as the total experience increases it may become more difficult to assimilate and accommodate to further experience. A state of equilibrium or ossification is reached which would be too much disturbed by new experiences of any depth and these are therefore rejected. Some people reach the stage quite early in life. Few escape it altogether.

To return to children, there are two points about the *schemata* which must be mentioned here. First they need exercising. Everyone is familiar with this truth at the adult stage. 'I used to play tennis a lot but now I can hardly hit a ball', 'I haven't read any Latin for years; I shouldn't understand a word now'. Remarks like that are often heard, but they generally refer to matters of marginal importance, or to activities which need the strength and vigour of youth for their performance. If they had been of major importance they would not have been forgotten. But with young children everything is important. They are learning about the world they live in, and they must be allowed to do things over and over again and thus reassure themselves that what they have learned is true; that patterns do repeat themselves, that things, if not people, are constant.

The other point about the *schemata* is that the exercise of them is pleasurable. Piaget has collected a lot of evidence that this is so, and indeed common observation would confirm it. Anyone who has watched a 2-year-old trying to fit two things together will have noticed the smile and the crow of delight when the task is accomplished. But many parents do not regard that sort of thing as learning. They think of it as play and as the child grows older and goes to school they contrast it with something different called work and sometimes grumble if, when he gets to school, the child is still 'allowed' to play. This business of play, and its contrast with work, now needs our attention.

Children have presumably played since the earliest days of man, but it was not until 1826, when Froebel published his *The Education of Man*, that the importance of play as a means of learning was first realised. Although all educationalists now recognise this importance, it is still little understood by the ordinary man and woman. Very few parents really watch children's play. Mothers will watch their babies when they are very young and play with their children when they are a little older. They will be in the room, or the garden or the park while the children are playing, but they will be sewing or knitting or cooking or talking to other mothers or to their husbands. They probably seldom watch closely and

systematically. Anyone who has done this will soon have
realised that play is much more than the release of surplus
energy. It is something undertaken with great seriousness
and concentration and is unmistakeably important to the
child. What is he doing as we watch him?

First of all and for much of the time he is clearly finding
out about materials—pouring water from one vessel to
another, squeezing a sponge, running it through a colander,
splashing it, using it to wet other things, sand or earth,
running sand or earth through his fingers, building it into
heaps, digging holes in it, piling bricks on each other,
knocking them down again, trying to lift or drag heavy
things, throwing light things into the air and watching them
float or fall to the ground again. These and countless other
similar kinds of play are the ways in which children discover
the nature of materials and begin to form concepts of weight,
height and breadth, texture, softness, hardness, plasticity,
impermeability, transparency and so on. In playing with
materials children begin also to discover the possibilities
and limitations of their own powers. They can reach some
things and not others. They can hold wet sand but dry sand
runs away. They can hold clay but not water. They can
destroy what they have made. They can break a stick but not
a log. This kind of play is an exploration of the physical world
and an attempt to discover how that world is related to the
child's own inner feelings. As soon as the matter is put like
that it begins to wear a rather unreal look, as it seems to
suggest a conscious effort on the part of a child to understand.
But the effort is not conscious in the sense that the child
says: 'Now I'm going to find out which of these two objects
is heavier'. That sort of approach to a problem comes later
on. In the early years children cannot give an account of what
they are doing. We can only deduce it from watching them
and we deduce that their play is an attempt to relate this
physical world to their own inner life. Anyone who grew up
without this ability would not survive for long. A knowledge
of the properties of materials, of how they behave in particular circumstances, is vital both in primitive and 'advanced'
societies.

It is equally important for children to understand people. They are surrounded by adults who control the greater part of their day and who themselves are occupied in all sorts of ways which the child sees and wants to understand. Once again, he does not know that this is what he wants, but his play makes it clear. He imitates the adults. He plays at being father and mother. Dolls and teddy-bears become children which he feeds, clothes, teaches and punishes. By this fantasy or pretending he begins to discover what it is like to be father or mother and thus to understand their behaviour. All the adults who impinge on his life tend to be imitated. Not only parents, but the milkman, the lorry-driver, the pilot, the doctor, the shopkeeper, the tractor-driver. And not only people. He will be a dog or a horse or a tiger he has seen at the zoo. His parents will probably have a clear role for him in their minds, an idea of how children *ought* to behave, of what they *ought* to be like. His play enables him to understand this role, but also to escape from it and, so to speak, to try other possibilities.

The situations that turn up in the child's life will also be dealt with by play. A painful situation—an accident, a death, a parting—will be repeated in play in order to make it more tolerable, in order that the child may 'live with it' as we say. Sometimes the situation is re-enacted many times and when this happens it is usually added to. More features, that were suppressed at the first enactment, are brought in, until the whole experience is brought into focus and control. This particular characteristic of play is often most clearly seen in child guidance clinics, when a child who is deeply disturbed will, over a period of time, play out the situation which is causing the trouble and, to that extent, cure himself.

Round about the end of the first year of life language begins to develop. This is an exciting moment for young parents. Their baby is at last going to be able to communicate with them, to *tell* them what he has been feeling and thinking all this time. They give him every encouragement. They report delightedly to grandparents and friends that he can now say 'seven words'. They have twinges of

anxiety when they hear that the child next door who is two
weeks younger can say 'twelve words'. They point to chickens
and say 'chook-chook' and they used to point to trains and
say 'puff-puff'. As language develops they talk to their
children, listen to them and converse with them. They do no
systematic teaching and yet when the child goes to school at 5,
he has nearly always performed the most difficult learning
feat of his whole life. He knows two or three thousand words
and he can speak fluently and clearly. How has this been
done?

Various influences have been at work. The parents have
encouraged, joined in, answered questions, read aloud,
corrected. When they have *not* done this the consequences
are painfully obvious. Sometimes a child turns up at school,
hardly able to speak at all or to understand anything but very
simple, short sentences and this nearly always reflects his
home. His parents may themselves be inarticulate or unintel-
ligent or they may be self-indulgent and neglectful. In either
case a vital condition of learning has been missing. The
influence of play is equally vital. The meanings of a great
many words can only be learned through play. If we watch
the play of children from 2 or 3 right on through the primary
school we shall notice how much language enters into it.
The meaning of a word is not usually an exact and limited
thing which, once learned, is fixed and complete. 'Father'
('Daddy') for instance, is the man who lives in the house,
who goes out in the morning and comes back for his tea, who
shares a bedroom with mummy, who mends things, who
looks after the car, who plays with him in a different way
from mummy, who sometimes gets very cross and irritable,
who comes home drunk, who is in prison, etc.,etc. All these
characteristics, if appropriate, will appear when the child
is playing at being father, and the words that stand
for them will be used and learned and their meanings,
so to speak, filled in. The same process occurs with
materials. The word 'water' is learned quite early, but its
full range of suggestion can only be learned through
play, through having discovered all the things that water
can and cannot do and the words: run, soak, drip, boil,

freeze, gurgle, splash, etc. which stand for those things.*

If all this is true of children before they reach school does it continue to be true afterwards, or does a quite new phase begin? Fifty years ago when a child entered the infants' school, he sat at a desk on his first day and he was taught and set tasks and kept there. There are many countries in the world where this still happens, though at a later age than 5. The implication is that when you get to school you put away childish things and begin lessons. It is perfectly true that school *is* a new phase of life and that most children expect to learn new things there, all the more so if they have grown up in happy and interesting homes. But the shock of separation from home even for a short day, and of finding oneself in a crowd of others, is, for many children, quite considerable, and there must be a period of assimilation and accommodation, before the new demands become insistent. Much more than that, however, the process of learning develops gradually and play continues to be of the greatest importance as a means of understanding and learning. If it is eliminated too soon the delight and pleasure of learning may go with it and drudgery take their place. Indeed the element of play is valuable in all work throughout life. Watch a man cultivating his garden and, whether he is doing it for a living or as a hobby, do you not detect an element in the work which can be properly called play? When that element is absent work becomes dull, repetitive, uninspiring and only worth doing because you make money by it. That is what D. H. Lawrence meant when he wrote: 'There is no point in work unless it absorbs you like an absorbing game, if it doesn't absorb you, if it's never any fun, don't do it!'[9]

We have been talking so far in this chapter almost as if teachers did not exist, as if all that was necessary for the education of children was intelligent parents and the right materials. It is perfectly true that the task of a teacher is much easier and much more productive if there is intelligent

---

* For a fuller treatment of the development of children's language and its connection with intellectual growth see Luria, A. R., and Yudovich, F. *Speech and the Development of Mental Process in the Child.* Staples Press, 1959.

co-operation from parents and that, given suitable material, children will learn a great deal without further adult aid. Put a 3-year-old down on a seashore, with sand and stones and rock-pools and you will not have to tell it what to do. I have intentionally emphasised this early stage of learning when the adult is the parent and when play is the chief means, because what goes on in the modern primary school cannot be understood without some knowledge of it. The teachers' role, however, is not less important than it used to be in the old days. It is more important. The skill, insight, imagination, initiative and range of knowledge that the modern approach requires in a teacher are much greater than those demanded in the old type of class teacher. In the next chapter it will be teachers that we shall be thinking about.

CHAPTER FOUR

Teachers

If you send your child to a maintained primary school* he will probably, but not certainly, be taught by a qualified teacher. The great majority of older qualified teachers have undergone a two-year course of training at what used to be called a Training College and is now called a College of Education. The younger teachers will have had a three-year course, because the course was lengthened in 1960. If one of the teachers has a University degree, he may have had no professional training at all, since, as a temporary measure during the shortage of teachers, the possession of a degree confers qualified status. He *may* have had a year's training at a University department of education or at one of a few colleges of education, or, if the degree is that of Bachelor of Education (B.Ed.) he will have had three years at a college of education, followed by an extra year of advanced work on which the B.Ed. is awarded. There may also be a teacher who was trained at one of the Emergency Training Colleges set up in 1945 to receive men from the Forces who wished to become teachers, and who were given an intensive one-year course. Finally, there are still a few older teachers who have been granted qualified status in recognition of long service even though they underwent no training when they were young.

If there are any unqualified teachers this will almost certainly be because of the difficulty, in the present shortage, of recruiting qualified ones. The unqualified teacher may be a young man or woman who is intending to go to a college of education and is gaining some practical experience first, or,

---

* People often call such schools 'state schools', but there are no state schools in England. The schools are maintained by Local Education Authorities and not by the Department of Education and Science.

where the shortage is very serious, any educated person who can be persuaded to fill the gap. It is perfectly reasonable for any parent to enquire about the qualifications of the teachers to whom he is entrusting his child, but do not too readily assume that an unqualified teacher must be a bad one. Some of them are very good indeed. It is also unwise to go to the other extreme and declare that 'qualifications don't matter since teachers are born not made.' A good course of training will make any teacher, however good, better.

A good course of training includes three main elements. First, it continues the education of the student as a person. He or she learns more about one or two subjects and continues studies begun in the sixth form. Secondly, it equips the student to teach certain subjects by thinking of their place in the school curriculum. Thirdly, it involves a study of the history and principles of education. Periods of teaching practice in schools during the training course ensure that what is learned in college is submitted to the test of practice and the problems met in school are discussed with the college teachers, and of course among the students themselves.

When a teacher has finished his course at a college of education he is not cut off from training or encouraged to regard himself as a 'finished product'. Various agencies exist which provide him with further training, guidance and inspiration. Some of these are described in Chapter Twelve. One, however, is perhaps most appropriately mentioned here, the institute or school of education. There are seventeen of these institutions in England, each attached to a university and every college of education is a member of one of them. They organise many different kinds of courses for serving teachers, some on a succession of winter evenings, some lasting for ten days or more during the summer vacation and some whole-time courses lasting for a year. These courses encourage teachers to maintain their interest, add to their knowledge and use their initiative and, although only a comparatively small proportion of teachers attend them, their influence on educational advance is substantial and on many individuals, crucial.

A young teacher beginning his career in a primary school

has had careful preparation and some experience. Opportunities will be open to him to enrich and deepen that experience and, in a good school, he will receive help and support from his head teacher and from his colleagues. He will almost certainly have general charge of a class and, if he is in a big school, he may teach some subject of which he has specialist knowledge, music or French or science perhaps, to others as well. Exactly what he does, how he does it and the amount that is left to him to decide will depend upon the kind of school he finds himself in. Some head teachers have very firm ideas about what they want and expect their staff to follow pretty closely the lines they have laid down. Others are more permissive. Some may leave too much to the individual. Most will steer a middle course.

What I want to sketch here is the role filled by a teacher in a school run on fairly up-to-date lines. He will first of all want to know the children as individuals. This takes a little time since it will not just be a matter of knowing their names, or even what they can do, but will mean getting to know them as people. This means establishing a relationship with them. Ideally this will be a relationship of mutual trust and respect, in which coercion and punishment have no place and where marks and rewards are unnecessary. Such a relationship is not always easy to establish and there may be individuals and sometimes whole groups with whom it is so difficult as to be practically impossible. But do not write it off as pie-in-the-sky. There are schools where it is the established relationship and many more in which at least something of it exists, and it is the ideal towards which very many teachers are striving. Where it exists a very favourable atmosphere for learning has been created. The children feel free and relaxed and at the same time, in the care of someone whom they respect and to whose authority they can trust themselves. It is not possible to reduce this sort of thing to a formula. Different teachers manage it in different ways. Some seem to be able to allow a much more permissive atmosphere, without the collapse of discipline, than others would find possible. Some need a firm framework of discipline in which to operate. It is a mistake to expect the same procedure from all, but the attitude is always unmistakeable.

In this atmosphere what does the teacher do? His first job is to see that the children have the materials that they need. If they are going to be allowed for some of the time to choose what they do there must be something to choose from. This does not mean simply making everything available. There must be a range of materials, which of course include books, suitable for the whole class, and a variety to satisfy individual needs. This is a skilled matter in itself. Furthermore, what is made available at any one moment is a matter for the teacher who has to use his judgement and often his ingenuity. To decide just when a child is ready to learn something new requires skill and experience. It is much easier to say 'children should begin reading when they are 5 or 5½ or 6', but that, as we saw in Chapter One, is to adopt a meaningless criterion.

The traditional method of teaching was to *give* a lesson and then test the children by questions spoken or written, or to *set* a lesson, i.e. give the children something to learn or do and then correct it. As an example of the former, we may take a lesson on the outbreak of the Civil War in which the teacher would outline the cause of the quarrel between the King and Parliament, and describe the events leading up to the break and would then ask and sometimes invite questions. An example of the second would be a chapter to read, or an English exercise or composition or a number of sums. Have these methods,with which most readers will be quite familiar, become out-of-date? Are they no longer found in the best primary schools?

The answer to these questions must, I am afraid, be 'Yes and No!' To take the given lesson first. There must always be a place for exposition by the teacher, for an account of something interesting and important in History or Science or Geography, but more teachers now do what the best teachers have always done. They do not so much give a lesson as lead a discussion, and they bring the children in and encourage them to comment and to ask questions as the 'lesson' proceeds. Discussion can be aimless, futile and a waste of time if every sort of irrelevance and personal opinion is allowed an airing. Here again it is the teacher who has the very skilled and exacting job of shaping the discussion and making it profitable. He must not be too quick to smell a red herring, or to discourage a silly question from a child who might then shut up like an oyster. Equally, he must not allow mere rambling and must keep the objective clear in his own mind and lead the discussion towards it. There is nothing fundamentally new in this method. It was used five hundred years before Christ by Socrates and is often called 'the Socratic method'. What is new is that it is being more and more extensively used in primary schools.

The *set* lesson too has a place. There must always be passages, or *formulae*, or constructions or arguments which must be committed to memory, and processes which must be practised. The difference between the old and the new approach may perhaps be best illustrated by reference to the multiplication table. The old-fashioned teacher set the children to learn the tables in order (2 to 12) by heart up to 144. When they knew what was strangely called *all* their tables—all that they really knew was up to 12×12—they were held to possess useful, indeed indispensable knowledge. The teacher's job in this was to set the task and to test the results. 'Until they know their tables,' he would say, 'they cannot make any progress'.

The modern teacher would agree that children must be taught to multiply, but he would approach it in a different way. To begin with, he would say that to know a table by heart is not to understand multiplication and he would try to help the children to 'build up', as the saying is, an understanding of the relationship between numbers before they do any memorising. He would certainly not take the tables in order or limit them to twelve times. He would show that the 4 and the 8 are only, so to speak, selections from the 2, the 6 and the 9 from the 3, and the 10 from the 5. He would show that the twelve is a selection from the 2, the 3, the 4 and the 6, and that the 7 and the 11 are the only odd men out. He would use a 10×10 grid and show the pattern made by each table in it and the relationships between them. He would, at every point, emphasise understanding as a stage that precedes memorisation.

The old-fashioned teacher might have objected to the new method on the grounds that it used up too much valuable time, but in fact the opposite is true as I will show from a personal experience. A nine-year-old child of my own received a report which simply ran: 'Does not know her tables'. On receiving the report I drew the table below on a piece of paper and proceeded to test her on it.

This I did by asking her each of the number bonds twice in random order, ticking off each answer as it came if it was right and putting a circle round the number if the answer was wrong, until I had covered the whole grid. This revealed that there were only six bonds that she did not know. She got each of them wrong both times and all the others right both times. It was therefore nonsense to say that 'she did not know her tables'; she knew nearly all of them! If the teacher had given this list to the whole class she would have discovered which bonds each child did not know and, thus, could have saved hours of their time and hers which they were spending

	2	3	4	5	6	7	8	9	10	11	12
1											
2	4	6	8	10	12	14	16	18	20	22	24
3	6	9	12	15	18	21	24	27	30	33	36
4	8	12	16	20	24	28	32	36	40	44	48
5	10	15	20	25	30	35	40	45	50	55	60
6	12	18	24	30	36	42	48	54	60	66	72
7	14	21	28	35	42	49	56	63	70	77	84
8	16	24	32	40	48	56	64	72	80	88	96
9	18	27	36	45	54	63	72	81	90	99	108
10	20	30	40	50	60	70	80	90	100	110	120
11	22	33	44	55	66	77	88	99	110	121	132
12	24	36	48	60	72	84	96	108	120	132	144

in memorising what they knew already. Any reader of this book whose child receives a similar report can try this simple test for himself and discover the true facts.

I have made rather a lot of this matter of tables, because it is the kind of thing that parents often worry about, and it illustrates very clearly the change in the teacher's role which has taken place in the modern primary schools. The old type

of teacher was all the time rather like an electric current.
When he was switched on something happened. When he was
switched off it stopped. The children had little chance of
showing initiative. The sums they worked, the compositions
they wrote, the poems they learned, the books they read, the
topics they studied were all chosen for them. They did what
they were told, and when they had finished they waited for
more or 'got out their readers'. Many of the teachers who
used this method were extremely skilful and the cleverest
children learned much from them, but it was nevertheless a
bad method, because it was so inflexible and because the
children seldom learned to work by themselves. It imposed a
pattern of learning on all the class and could make little
allowance for individual differences.

The new type of teacher plays a much more variable role.
If you go into his classroom you may find him standing before
the class and teaching them, but you are just as likely to find
the class busily occupied with a variety of different things—
books, writing, painting, mathematics, science—inside the
classroom and out, while the teacher moves about among
them, answering questions and asking them, offering
encouragement, making suggestions, correcting mistakes,
helping with difficulties, solving problems. The children are
supplying their own current. They are wasting far less time
and doing much more work, than under the old system. So
is the teacher! Do not be under any delusion about that.
The new methods make very heavy demands on the patience,
good humour, energy, knowledge and skill of the teacher,
but it is also true to say that they are much more rewarding
for him as well as for the children. They learn much from
him but he learns from them too. Their inventiveness and
creativeness are released and they will ask him questions to
some of which he does not know the answer off-hand. He
can never fall back on a dull routine. The children are
always stimulating him to make new discoveries. He may be
dog-tired at the end of the day but he will never be bored.

There will be some readers who at this point will ask:
'Isn't this all a bit starry-eyed?' I must remind them that in
Chapter One I promised to describe the schools which are

in the van of progress and not those which are in the rear.
I have been a teacher myself and I have had the privilege of
meeting thousands of teachers and seeing them at work. I
know a lot about the rewards and delights of teaching as well
as about its setbacks and disappointments. I have experienced
the periods when everything goes with a swing and the
periods when everything seems to stick. I have known
difficult children, difficult classes, difficult schools and
difficult areas, as well as dull and incompetent teachers. For
a third of a century I have worked in the primary schools of
England. What I have described above is of course not
universal, but it is not so exceptional as to be misleading and
it is becoming commoner. In some areas it is indeed the
commonest pattern, in few is it non-existent.

The dominating influence in every school is that of the
head teacher. Legally the curriculum of a school is the
responsibility of the local education authority, but in
practice L.E.A.s delegate this responsibility to head
teachers. An imaginative and gifted Head can transform a
school despite a fairly mediocre staff, whereas an enterprising
assistant teacher has very limited scope if the Head Teacher
is unsympathetic.

The head teacher is appointed by the Managers of the
School. If it is a voluntary aided school, that is a Church
School which has retained its old status, two-thirds of the
managers will be a self-appointing body, usually with the
parish priest, Anglican or Roman Catholic, as chairman, with
a representative of the L.E.A. sitting with them. If the school
is a Voluntary Controlled School, that is a Church School
which has surrendered some of its independence in return
for financial assistance, only one-third of the managers will
be appointed by the Church but will still usually be under
the chairmanship of the incumbent. If the school is a
County School, that is a school provided and maintained by
the L.E.A., the managers will be appointed by the L.E.A.
and the arrangements for the choice of head teacher will be
entirely in the L.E.A.s hands. The post will be advertised
locally and, usually, nationally and anyone may apply. This
is the usual procedure, but a few large L.E.A.s have a list of

candidates for early promotion and appointments to headships are made only from this list.

Once he is appointed, a head teacher is given almost complete freedom in deciding how his school is to be run. The curriculum, i.e. the range of subjects taught, is to a large extent determined by custom. It is not prescribed, and if the head teacher wants to add or drop a subject, for example a foreign language, he is, in practice, free to do so, though, as was stated earlier, the L.E.A. have the legal right to overrule him, whilst the Department of Education and Science and H.M. Inspectors have none. The methods of teaching, the time-table, the balance of subjects, the text-books and the books in the library, the methods of discipline, are all the Head Teacher's responsibility and he can decide whether to run his school democratically and consult his staff at all points or autocratically and issue instructions and schemes to them. The general climate of opinion is of course democratic and in practice the great majority of schools are run on a more or less democratic basis. Nevertheless the head teacher is not simply 'first among equals'. He is responsible for the running of his school and he has the right and the power to run it as he thinks best. In the last resort the staff must carry out his wishes, and if they do not agree with them must seek other posts.

In no other country in the world is so much responsibility put on the head teacher, or, of course, so much liberty of decision given to him. We shall see, in Chapter 12, what devices exist to try to ensure that the responsibility is not too heavy and the liberty not abused. For the moment, the question is what actually happens in a school when this system is working happily. Most readers will guess the answer to this. Dr. H. M. Butler, who was Headmaster of Harrow School from 1859 to 1885, once called his staff together and put before them a proposal for a change of policy which would affect the whole life of the school. In the discussion which followed it emerged that the staff were strongly and unanimously against what the headmaster proposed. He finally terminated it with these words: "I thank you gentlemen for this frank expression of your opinion and I shall adopt the course of action that I have in mind with the greater regret". No headmaster of any school in England could now do that and few would wish to. There were many such figures fifty years ago, male and female, in every kind of school, but their day is past, and the head and his staff now work together and all important changes are not only discussed but usually agreed upon. In some staff-rooms the atmosphere is more relaxed than in others and an unsympathetic, or tactless head teacher can still, of course, make an unhappy or divided staff. No system perhaps could make such a development impossible. But generally staffs are friendly and co-operative and on easy terms with their head teacher.

It is very important that they should be so. Disgruntled or unhappy teachers will not teach well, and a 'bad atmosphere' in the staff-room infects the whole school and is quickly sensed by the children. Relaxed, flexible yet purposeful methods in the classroom derive in part from the climate on the staff, and for this the head teacher is mainly responsible.

A parent who is about to send his child to school for the first time will be anxious, above all perhaps, that he should have 'good teachers'. Most parents have in practice little choice of school. Their child must go to the nearest school whatever it is like. For this reason, among many others, the State tries to ensure that there are 'good teachers' in every school, and that schools which fall below good standards are helped to raise themselves. The training system, the innumerable courses for serving teachers, the L.E.A.s with their organisers, the Department with H.M. Inspectors, are all concerned with raising standards and the teachers' organisations are continuously and widely concerned with the same object. The fact remains, however, that, despite all these agencies, some schools and some teachers remain obstinately better than others. It is difficult to imagine any state of affairs in which this would not be so, or any kind of social engineering which could eliminate it. Even the despairing step of cutting everything down to a supposedly common level would only reproduce the same disparities shorn of excellence. Parents must accept a considerable element of luck in the quality of the teachers their children get. The important thing is to co-operate with the teachers to the greatest possible extent with the benefit of all the children as the common objective.

The curriculum, the time-table and organisation

We have already seen in Chapter 4 that the curriculum, though legally under the control of the Local Education Authority, is in fact the responsibility of the Head Teacher. We must now look a little more closely at it. Many foreign visitors find it almost incredible that we should leave this essential matter to personal taste. In the Iron Curtain countries, of course, the curriculum and the text-book are exactly prescribed and virtually no deviation from either allowed. But in the countries of the west too, including the U.S.A., there is far more central or state control over the choice of subjects and the syllabus to be followed than in England, and to some it appears that we are almost in a state of anarchy. The freedom and the resultant responsibility are real, but they are not quite as unlimited as might first appear.

The basic legal control is simply Clause 36 of the Education Act of 1944, which states: 'It shall be the duty of the parent of every child of compulsory school age to cause him to receive efficient full-time education suitable to his age, ability and aptitude . . .'. The matter has never come into the courts, but it must be presumed that if a head teacher was so eccentric as to omit for instance any trace of mathematics in his syllabus, he or the L.E.A. could be prosecuted for preventing the parents of the children from carrying out their obligations. This possibility is, of course, a piece of pure fantasy. An effective control until recently has perhaps been the 11 + examination, which exercised a normalising influence on the primary school curriculum. This control will disappear as comprehensive secondary education increases, though the demands, supposed or expressed, of the secondary schools will continue to have some influence in the primary schools. Probably the strongest control of all is simply that of custom. The curriculum of the old elementary school was originally (see Chapter One) what was considered necessary and advisable for the children of the working class. Gradually it was widened, but between 1900 and 1960 it scarcely altered at all. Religious instruction, arithmetic, English, history, geography, nature study, art, music, craft (boys), needlework (girls), physical education. It was rare to find a school in those sixty years which omitted any of these or included anything else. If the same sort of classification is used, the curriculum of a modern primary school would include only one additional subject—a modern language—and that would only be true of one in five. Arithmetic would be called Mathematics, Nature Study would be called Science and there would not be a sharp division between Craft for boys and Craft for girls. There would be many internal differences and the whole curriculum would be looked at very differently but the actual *list of subjects* would, a modern language apart, be recognisably the same. There would be little disagreement that these subjects in some form or other should form part of a good general education. The curriculum in that sense is likely to remain much the same for as long as can be imagined.

In the following chapters I shall describe and discuss the curriculum under headings which group some of the traditional subjects together, but which in the main follow them. This is the most convenient way of dealing with them. But a comparison between the time-table that was typical of the old pre-1944 elementary school and that which is found in a modern primary school, will show that the curriculum is now something very different from what it used to be.

The old time-table was divided into compartments which showed exactly what was to be done by each class at every moment of the day. After 30 minutes of religious instruction there followed, almost invariably, 45 or even 50 minutes of arithmetic. English occupied most of the rest of the morning. This was often sub-divided into spelling, grammar, recitation, speech training, reading, composition and dictation, each with its allotted time. The other subjects were treated in the same way. In practice there was often rather more flexibility than the time-table suggested and the Head Teacher always had powers to vary or change it. It had to be signed by H.M.I. This was intended to show only that it complied with the law covering religious instruction (i.e. that this should be either at the beginning or end of a session, so that children who were withdrawn on conscientious grounds could be more conveniently provided for). Unfortunately the signature was sometimes taken as indicating inspectorial approval for the whole time-table and even as an obstacle to changes made without H.M.I.'s approval. For this reason many inspectors in the 1930s refused to sign time-tables even though it was part of their duties.

It was the infants' schools which began the breakaway from the rigid time-table. It became increasingly clear to teachers that such a time-table was totally unsuited to all that was known about the nature of young children and the way in which they learned. But the change came rather slowly. In many country schools the infants were taught by untrained teachers who were sometimes timid about innovations and preferred definite guiding-lines. When the change was made it often consisted only of rather more general headings, still blocked out in precise periods of time—number, reading, activities, written work, oral work, craft and so on. In the junior schools or upper classes of full-range primary schools the change came even more slowly. No head teacher of such a school could entirely ignore the 11+ examination and many felt themselves obliged to let it influence the work of the school sometimes to a very marked degree. It was all very well, perhaps, to have free time-tables in the infants' schools but time was short and once the children were seven they must 'get down to it'. So the argument ran and 'getting down to it' meant a clearly mapped-out day. Many parents, perhaps the majority, agreed with this and sometimes head teachers with more progressive ideas met with grumblings and complaints from that quarter.

Quite apart from these objections to a flexible time-table, there were some plain practical difficulties. In all but the smaller schools there would probably be some specialisation. A good musician would naturally and properly take the music of more than his own class. Needlework would be taught by a woman and mainly only to girls. The hall, if there was one, would have to be used for physical education at allotted times. If the children went outside for anything, to a swimming bath or to a distant playing-field, this would have to be exactly time-tabled. These difficulties obviously still apply and even in the most permissive schools nowadays there are fixed points on the time-table at various times in the day. Apart from these, however, it is becoming increasingly common for the rest of the day to be left entirely to the individual teacher's discretion, to decide when any particular subject is to be studied and how much time is to be spent on it.

How does this work out in practice? Is there not a danger that some things will be neglected and others over-stressed, perhaps according to the teacher's preferences or whims? How can continuity and cohesion be assured? These questions will undoubtedly occur to most readers and, when it is added that the children are likely to be working individually and, for some of the time, be doing quite different things from each other, there may be doubts aroused as to whether the whole thing is not something near the chaos that many foreign visitors suspect.

I have already said (page 41) that the new approach makes heavier and not lighter demands upon the skill of the teacher. It will be obvious that the flexible time-table is also a great test of his skill and that a careful record has to be kept of what each child does so as to ensure that over a period, say of a term, there is a proper balance between subjects and appropriate progress within subjects. Part of this record will consist of the child's own work. If each child has a folder in which all his written work, in whatever subject, is kept, it will be possible to see quite rapidly whether both these requirements are being met. The teacher will also maintain his own records and these two together will constitute a much more informative and useful account of work done than the old type of teacher's record which was simply a statement of lessons given and set.

Parents need then have no fear that the new approach and the free time-table necessarily lead to chaos, but they may well ask whether, admitting that they make heavy demands on the skill of the teacher, they have enough positive advantages over the old to be worth it. Part of the answer to that question has already been given in Chapters 2 and 3. The differences between children and the ways in which they learn are all best suited by an individual and flexible programme. But what about the subject matter that they learn? What about sheer 'knowledge'? Is there not a danger of just playing about with a subject to the neglect of sound learning? In mathematics, for example, which is very 'structured', that is, something in which the parts must be fitted together in a logical order, this danger might be considerable. A smattering of a modern language might be given instead of a solid foundation. A vague interest in the past might be aroused without any corresponding sense of historical development. The end product might be someone who has flitted about like a butterfly without ever mastering anything, who expects to have things made interesting and easy for him without having to take much trouble himself, who has never learned how to concentrate or how to work hard. Such fears are often expressed and I must try to dissipate them.

First it must be clearly understood that no method is foolproof. Just as the traditional method could and did produce dullness and waste of time, so the new methods could produce just the results that people fear. No method is better than the teacher who is using it. A poor teacher will make a mess of any method, and a good teacher will make a success of any. But that is not to say that the method does not matter and that all you need is a good teacher. A method which takes account both of the nature of children and of the subject-matter concerned will be better in good hands than a method which fails to do this in the same hands. Further, though no method will make a good teacher out of a bad one, a good method will encourage an ordinary teacher to persevere and to learn more, while a bad one will too easily turn him into an automaton. Drained of any idealism he once had, cynical and repressive, such a teacher is a blight on any staff, but so of course is the type who climbs on every new bandwaggon without understanding what it is or where it is going to. Fortunately, though these two types exist and may be known to readers, they are not characteristic of the profession as a whole. Most teachers are anxious to do their best for their children. and to improve their knowledge and their techniques with that purpose in view. If they adopt a new method they do it because it seems to them a good one and because they feel able to cope with it. A parent who finds that his child is being educated in a way that startles him ought to begin by assuming that the teachers know what they are doing and only complain when he has some clear evidence that they don't.

Secondly, the subdivision of learning and knowledge into subjects needs a little consideration. A 4-year-old who is told a story is not concerned with whether it is history, legend, myth, parable or fiction. He is concerned simply with whether it is a good story or not. The *kind* of story that it is may interest him later on and be of great importance to him, but not at 4 years old. A 9-year-old who writes an account of an experiment in science which has involved some measurement and calculations, does not think: 'Now I am doing English, now science and now mathematics', though all three are involved. A class of 10-year-olds in the course of a visit to a local church may be interested in matters which might properly be classified as history (when and why the church was built), religion (the altar and the rood-screen), geology (the stone used and where it came from), engineering (how the church was built), mathematics (the weight and density of the materials), science (the effect of weather on the materials), campanology (the ring of bells in the tower), entomology (the death-watch beetle in the rafters), to name only some. The children do not make this classification in their minds. It is all part of their visit to the church. The classification is of course useful, but its usefulness is limited, and it may even be a hindrance. An entomologist who knows no botany will not get far. Young children simply do not think in this way and only begin to use classification towards the end of the junior school. A rigidly classified time-table ('No Susan! we're doing history now, not art') may be harmful to learning and may disguise the nature of knowledge.

In the following chapters I am going to classify the subjects more or less in the usual way, because, for adult readers, that is the most familiar and convenient way of dealing with them, though the way in which some of these are presented is unusual. Again and again it will be clear that in the classroom this classification breaks down and that there are no barriers between one subject and another.

If what has been said about how children grow and learn and about how the curriculum is put together has been followed, it will be no surprise that the internal organisation of the school is liable to be very different from what it used to be. Until the new Code of 1926 children were grouped in Standards, which were much the same as the American Grades. You stayed in Standard 1 until you had covered its syllabus satisfactorily and were then promoted to Standard 2 and so on. It was then not uncommon to find slow or supposedly stupid children of 12 still trying to get out of Standard 2 and miserably repeating the same work year after year. This was succeeded by promotion by age. Children moved up each year regardless of their achievement. It was argued that they would have to live and compete with their contemporaries after they had left school and that they had better begin at once. This arrangement made it more difficult to teach classes as a whole, so the custom grew up of dividing them into groups—fast, medium, slow—for reading and arithmetic. Many teachers showed great skill in handling this group-organisation but it often led to a great waste of time. The slow groups suffered because they could not get on without the teacher, and the fast groups, though they could do this, were deprived of the teacher's attention and stimulus while he was helping the slow ones.

It was this disadvantage which led to the introduction of streaming. In schools which were big enough the age-groups were streamed, so that there was an A stream and a B stream and in a few very large primary schools a C stream. This, it was hoped, would make it possible for children to go at their own pace, without being either held back by the needs of those slower than themselves or discouraged by the invariable superiority of those who were faster. In the 1930s this organisation was almost universally approved, but it was obviously only possible in schools with a 2-form entry. An enormous number of primary schools were, and still are, too small for streaming and have always had to manage without it. It must also be said that streaming did not remove the necessity for grouping, though it did make it possible to match the speed of progress more closely to the individual.

Streaming is now a matter of great controversy.[10] What was introduced as a liberal measure to help both children and teachers is now attacked as being a denial of social equality and as educationally unsound. It is a difficult question to discuss coolly. The arguments in its favour are the obvious ones which have already been given and to these must be added another. The research undertaken by the National Foundation for Educational Research on behalf of the Department of Education and Science has revealed that in terms of measurable achievement, children in streamed schools do a little better, though not much, than children in unstreamed schools. If that were the only consideration we might decide in favour of streaming without further argument, but measureable achievement is not the only thing that has to be taken into account, and it is therefore necessary to look at the arguments on the other side.

The first of these is that children who find themselves in a lower stream are treated by teachers as being permanently second-rate, that they acquire a lower stream mentality and tend to under-rate themselves and, as a protection, profess to despise the A stream and their interests as snobbish. This attitude is reinforced by the undoubted fact that the A stream tends broadly to be more middle-class than the B stream. Streaming, it is held, perpetuates class differences and makes it difficult if not impossible for all children to realise their potential. It is divisive and wasteful.

The second argument against streaming is that it overlooks the extent to which children can learn from each other. In an unstreamed class, that is one in which all the varying abilities in the age-group are present, the slow learn from the quick and the quick learn from helping the slow. In a small village school this has always happened and it is in such schools that some of the most interesting and advanced work is found. In some infants' schools this arrangement is carried even further. The school is not merely unstreamed. It is unclassified altogether. Each class is a complete cross-section of the school and includes all ages as well as all abilities, a system known as vertical or family grouping.

It must be said at once that both unstreaming and family grouping are matters of considerable disagreement not only among primary teachers generally but also among those who may be broadly classified as progressive. A diminishing number of infant schools stream but only a tiny minority adopt family grouping. A large majority of junior schools retain streaming in the third and fourth years but it is becoming increasingly common to abandon it in the first two years, and there is a growing tendency to do so in the third. The evidence is that teacher-opinion, though still in favour of streaming, anyhow in the later primary years, is moving fairly rapidly towards unstreaming as a general policy.

It may seem at first sight as if this trend means a return to the situation that succeeded 'standards', to the 'group-system' which was described above, and which proved so unsatisfactory that it led to streaming, in fact that the wheel has come full-circle. But this is not really so. The old group-system functioned in an era of class-teaching, when the emphasis was on the given and set lesson, when little scope existed for initiative by the children, when the areas of teaching were a good deal more limited, and the materials of learning very limited indeed. If unstreaming is introduced today it will nearly always be in a school in which there is a training in independence, scope for initiative and choice, opportunities for experiment and first-hand experience of many kinds and in which the teacher's role is varied in the way described on pages 41-42.

It is too early to say whether this trend towards un-streaming and family grouping will accelerate or slow down. As experience of the results grows teachers will be better able to make up their minds, and in doing this they will have the findings of researchers to help or hinder them. Here, as everywhere else in education, the personality of the teacher counts for so much that it is dangerous to lay down the law. What was said above (page 49) about method is equally true of organisation. If you think your child has a good teacher—good in every sense you can think of—do not worry overmuch about methods or organisations.

CHAPTER SIX

English
A. LEARNING TO READ

If you were to go into a class of five-year-olds in a modern infants' school, or into any class in an infants' school organised in family groups, and ask how the children are taught to read, you might receive one of several answers. This most vital matter, like everything else, with the exception of Religious instruction, is left in the hands of the teacher. There are various methods of teaching reading—the alphabetic (now almost obsolete), the phonetic, the look-and-say or whole-word method and the sentence method. In practice the majority of infants' schools use a combined look-and-say and phonetic method and it is this that I am going to describe.

In the Fives' classroom you would probably see a number of words and sentences in various places in the room, The door would have the word 'door' fastened on it and the window the word 'window'. The sentences might be about the weather, e.g. 'the sun is shining' (this would be changed to suit the conditions outside), or about the children, e.g. 'Simon has a new baby sister', or about a story that had been read or told to the children, e.g. 'The little red hen cleaned the house'. If you searched further you would find cards with words and sentences written on them and readers which began with very simple sentences like 'This is Peter' under a picture of a little boy, and went on to more extended sentences in later books. You would very likely find books made by the children of previous years containing pictures and words and sentences, and also a good variety of picture books, that is books to look at and learn about things from.

The aim of all this material is to allow the children to get used to printed words, to the look of them, to associating

them with what they stand for. The children will have been
speaking and hearing words since they were a year old and,
by the time they come to school they can usually converse
quite fluently and use, (though estimates vary) on the
average, about 2,000 different words. All this they have
learned without any formal teaching. It is generally believed
that it is unwise to try to teach them to read until they have
reached a fair state of proficiency with spoken language,
and that the early stages of reading should be quite informal.

In the classroom described above, the children become
accustomed to printed words. They look at what they 'say'.
The teacher draws their attention to them. In many schools
they learn to read them by writing them. This is really only a
small extension of what goes on at home. 'What does that
notice say, mummy?' asks the child and the mother replies:
'It says Private—No entry'. 'What does private mean? Why
is it private? What would happen if we went in?' The
questions follow in quick succession. No attempt is made to
teach them reading but next time they pass the notice the
child says: 'There's the private notice' and soon the word
private is recognised. In school this process is taken a little
further because, though it is informal and may look casual,
it is in fact deliberate. The infants' teacher will actively
encourage a curiosity about words and, when she thinks the
children are ready, will use the cards mentioned above,
'flash-cards' as they are called, to give training in quick
recognition of whole words and sentences.

Some children are so quick at learning that they go on
under their own steam so to speak and learn to read almost
without further teaching. Such children are not only naturally bright, but they usually have the advantage of parents
who talk to them, answer their questions, provide them with
plenty of books and are themselves 'great readers'. The
majority of children however will need more help and some a
great deal more. When they can recognise something like 200
words by this look-and-say method and read them in short
phrases or sentences, they are ready for the phonetic stage.
English is not a phonetically spelt language. Its spelling is
extremely erratic, so much so that precisely the same

combination of letters may have different sounds in different words. It is no use trying to teach a child to read 'cough', 'rough', 'thought', 'drought', 'though' and 'thorough' by means of the sounds of letters. Such words can only be learned by recognition of the whole word. In many words, however, combinations of letters do correspond more or less closely to particular sounds. Most of the words in that last sentence are of this kind. Words such as 'however', 'correspond' 'or', 'less' and 'particular' can be tackled on a phonetic basis. 'In', 'many', 'words', 'of', 'do', 'more', 'closely' and 'to'—though the sounds of the vowels are not consistent, are nevertheless likely to be correctly read with a phonetic approach. It may also work with 'sounds' although the diphthong 'ou' is not consistent as witness 'wounds' 'rough' 'pour', etc. The advantage of this phonetic method is that it gives to children a reasonably efficient instrument for tackling a new and unfamiliar word. Here, as in look-and-say, the quick children will make better progress than the slow ones. A slow child, faced with 'particular', may sound it out slowly and with difficulty 'par-tick-you-lar' and even not immediately grasp what the whole word is. A quick child will probably get it before the sounding process is complete 'par-tick-you—oh I see! "p'tickulah"'.

In the process of learning to read there is a sort of frontier. Once a child is over it, the main job is done. He may still need help, but he can read. He can, as teachers say, get on by himself. For some children the approach to this frontier is very slow and some seem to hang about just on the wrong side of it for quite a long time. They need continual help and support. It is possible that some children of this kind have been started on reading too early. They have found it a struggle and have had little pleasure from it. They would perhaps have done better if they had been allowed to remain for longer in the pre-reading stage, getting used to printed words without formal instruction. We know (see Chapter 2) that it is futile to try to teach children to stand or walk before they are ready, when they do it without being taught, and it is very probable that the same thing is true of reading.

Nevertheless reading is so important and so essential a means to education that it is not surprising that parents and teachers worry about children who find it difficult or are very slow starters. The proportion of children who cannot read when they leave the primary school is so small that it is not, nationally, a problem though that does not make it any less of a handicap to the children concerned. But a rather larger proportion—perhaps as high as 15%—are poor readers[11] and will go on to their secondary schools with very limited reading powers. How can this problem be tackled?

If the Plowden Report's recommendation that the age-range of the infants' school should be extended to 8 be adopted, some of the trouble will disappear. Teachers trained specially for work in infants' schools are generally the best teachers of reading, while those who are trained for junior work tend to feel that the job of teaching reading ought to have been finished before the children reach them and even to resent slightly the task of coping with non-readers and backward readers. An extra year in the infants' school will make all the difference to children of this kind.

Various attempts have been made over the years to ease the process of learning to read by the use of different colours to represent different sounds, by supplying the children with typewriters, by using very large type, and so on. The device which has attracted the most attention in this country and which, alone, has been extensively tried out in English schools, is the Initial Teaching Alphabet invented by the late Isaac Pitman and perfected by his grandson, Sir James Pitman.[12] The argument on which this invention is based is that the English alphabet, originally adopted by Caxton from Latin, is so hopelessly inconsistent in its relationship to sounds as to present a formidable obstacle to the learning of reading by children. Not only does it suffer from this inconsistency but it is made worse by there being two or three quite different forms for many of the letters, e.g. A a *a*, B b *b*, D d, E e, F f *f*, G g *g*, H h, I i, J j, L l, M m, N n, P p, Q q, R r, T t, Y y, Z z. The I.T.A. abolishes these differences and for capital letters uses simply an enlarged form of the 'small' letter. More important, instead of 24

letters it uses 44, and each of these 44 letters represents only
one sound, so that a child never has to face the innumerable
exceptions to every rule that are given to him in T.O.
These letters stand for Traditional Orthography, which is
simply the way that words are spelt and printed in this book.

I.T.A., when it was first proposed, was greeted with much
scepticism and even hostility and this has not yet completely
disappeared. It was said that the children would find the new
letters (only 20 of them were different from the ordinary
forms) difficult to learn. In fact they learned them just as
quickly as they had learned the old ones, and even adults,
who found it harder because they were used to the old ones,
in fact grew accustomed to the new alphabet in an hour or so.
It was said that children who had learned I.T.A. would
find it difficult to switch to T.O. later on. It has been found
that they have no difficulty whatever. These two objections
were easily disposed of. There were others, however, which
were more solid. One was a technical objection made by
some experts in phonetics who pointed out that there are
many more sounds in the English language than I.T.A. can
cope with. This is perfectly true. An alphabet which had one
sign for every possible subtlety of sound in English would
run to hundreds of letters. No one in fact has yet determined
how many different phonemes there are in this language.
But this point is quite irrelevant to the learning of reading.
The essential thing is that the alphabet should be consistent,
not that it should differentiate every sound.

A much more relevant objection was that if most children
learned to read satisfactorily with T.O. the expense of
providing books printed in I.T.A. in the interests of a small
minority was not justifiable. The sponsors of I.T.A. claim
that although it is the backward readers who make the most
spectacular progress with I.T.A., all children learn to read
more quickly and easily than with T.O. and that the time
thus saved and made available for other things is worth the
expense involved.

The verdict must ultimately depend on whether the claims
made turn out to be justified. The research which has been
going on since 1961 under the auspices of the University of

London and with financial support from D.E.S. is not yet complete. About 10% of English infants' schools[13] are known to be using the I.T.A. (N.B. It *is* an alphabet *not* a method). The results so far appear to support the claims and many schools which have adopted I.T.A. have continued its use and are enthusiastic about its results. To some it may seem that the opponents of I.T.A. are fighting a last ditch battle. This may in fact be so, but the history of education is packed with bright ideas and gimmicks for which vast claims have been made and which have either disappeared without trace or been absorbed into general practice and taken a much smaller place in it than their inventors hoped. Teachers are right to be cautious. Nevertheless I must give it as my personal opinion that the evidence is convincing and I have yet to see any or to hear any argument which decisively points to an unfavourable verdict.

When the reading frontier is crossed the real excitement of books begins. From the very start, as we have seen, the modern primary school surrounds children with books so that they may make friends with them and regard them as something of major importance. This was not always so. I can remember infants' classes where the only reading matter was grubby and tattered primers, and junior classes in which there was little beside text-books and school readers. In the last twenty years there has been a welcome change. The publishers have issued an enormous quantity of attractive children's books. The D.E.S. has done much to encourage a generous policy in the supply of books and most L.E.A.'s have greatly increased the book allowance.

In the Sixes and Sevens classes you will find a quantity of books. They will probably be scattered about the room, on various shelves or sometimes in a little library corner. They will certainly not be locked away in cupboards. The children will be able to get hold of them whenever they need them. Many of the books will be simple, illustrated introductions to a variety of interests and topics—aeroplanes, space-flight, railways, motor-cars, ships, houses, plants, birds, insects. There will also be some rather larger books of reference. Even at this age children often want to know more

about a subject than a brief child's book can tell. There will
also be story-books, books of poetry, collections of myths and
legends from all over the world, and books about the Holy
Land and the Life of Our Lord.

The use made of these books will vary. Some the children
will borrow and take home with them to read. Some they will
choose for themselves, some try at their teacher's suggestion.
Some will be read simply for the immediate pleasure they
give, some to discover the answer to a question or to settle an
argument. Increasingly as the children grow older the books
will be used in close connection with their studies. I once
visited a little country school in Yorkshire where the children,
under the headmaster's direction, had excavated the site of a
mediaeval village. I shall return to this school in a later
chapter. What I want to mention here is the shelf of books
borrowed from the County Library, which the children were
using. These were not children's books at all. They were
books about local history and topography, books about
mediaeval houses, customs and implements, parish records,
church accounts and so on. This was reading with a purpose
and it was interesting to see what difficult and sometimes dull
and long passages the children would tackle when they contained information that they really needed.

This lavish provision of books and their constant use has
perhaps been the most striking change in the English primary
school since the war. Until it happened the full possibilities
of children using their own initiative could not be realised or
even imagined. In every subject teachers have been surprised
at how much children will do when given a chance, and the
chance is so often a good supply of good books.

B. BOOKS FOR CHILDREN

In the last section I described briefly the sort of books that you will find in a modern primary school. In the course of doing this I emphasised the great advantage possessed by children whose parents provided them with books, read to them and discussed with them what they had read. In no other subject of the curriculum is the participation and co-operation of parents more important. The head teacher of an infants' school in a new town recently told me that most of the children arrived in school at 5, quite unable to listen to a story. They were unable because they had had no experience of listening at home. They had never been told a story or been read to by their mothers. People who live in new towns are faced with a lot of expense and often have high standards in the matter of houses, clothing, food, cars and holidays. It is understandable that the mothers should want, or be obliged, to contribute to the family income. If, however, this means that they have no time to read to their . children, to tell them stories and to talk to them, they are depriving them of an important, perhaps of an essential part of their education, and making nonsense of their ambitions for them. A good school can do something to make up for the deficiencies of a home, but it is uphill work and there is a good deal that it cannot do.

For this reason, I am, in this section, going rather more fully into children's reading, with a view to helping parents to choose books for their children and to co-operate with the schools. Books can be considered under five heads:

1. Books for information;
2. Folk-lore and legend;
3. Children's classics;

4. Modern books;

5. Poetry.

1. BOOKS FOR INFORMATION. On the whole books of this kind are well represented in schools and good use is made of them there. When a child shows an interest in something, whether it be aeroplanes, railways, stamps or butterflies, the most important thing is for his parents to encourage the interest by sharing it if possible and by listening to what he has to say about it. If the interest is to be maintained and developed it will need the support of books. Here the children's department of the public library will be the first source to tap but soon the child will want his own books. I well remember the thrill of being given Coleman's *British Butterflies* (the price was 3s. 6d. then) when I was nine and the even greater one of being promoted to South's *Butterflies of the British Isles* when I was eleven. The possession of one's own copy of whatever it is is a great step forward and one that should always be encouraged. But there are many expensive and worthless books on the market and before money is laid out, the advice of the children's Librarian or of some friend who happens to share the child's interest should always be sought.

2. FOLK-LORE AND LEGEND. Long before anything was written down, let alone printed, stories were made and told. They were passed down by word of mouth from generation to generation, and they spread all over the world, so that a story told in New Guinea may be recognisably the same as one told by the peasants in Moldavia. There are many collections of these stories, myths and legends of Rome and Greece, of Scandinavia, of Mexico and Peru, of the American-Indians, of the Celtic races, folk-tales from all over the world. It is a pity to call them fairy tales because this suggests sentimental, flimsy-winged creatures which modern children rightly despise, but one of the best collections, those made by the late Andrew Lang, do in fact have this in their title— *The Blue Fairy Book*, the *Red Fairy Book*, etc. These old stories still appeal to children and for a very definite reason. The situations they describe, the characters they contain are ones of fundamental importance and interest to human

beings. Think of all the stories about the prince changed into
a monster by evil spells and only restored to his proper
shape when the princess overcomes her repulsion and
kisses him. This story is found in every part of the world.
It is a sort of parable about love and sex. The romantic lover
is a young girl's dream and quite unreal. The thought of
physical love is repellent to her. Only when the two are
combined and seen to be part of one whole can she find
happiness. The prince and the monster are the same person.
When a little girl reads the story of *Beauty and the Beast*
she does not consciously realise that this is what it is about,
nor do we tell her, but it may well be that this old primitive
way of introducing the facts of life to children in the form of
stories which disguised them, was a very good one and
showed far more sense than our embarrassed and clinical
methods of modern sex-instruction. Many of the stories, of
course, are simply parables of nature. The rape of Proserpine
and the promise that, though she had to spend six months
underground in the dark kingdom of Pluto, she might return
for the other six to the sunlight and her mother Ceres, is the
story of corn cut down in the autumn and springing up again
as the days lengthen. This was a magical process to the
primitive mind and it was natural to explain it in terms of
gods and goddesses. It is no less wonderful because we can
now describe it in scientific terms and children can still
enjoy the legend and perhaps appreciate the wonder more
readily through it, than through the explanation that they
will quite early in life demand and need.

3. CHILDREN'S CLASSICS. There are some books which have
established themselves as firm favourites and which seem,
sometimes surprisingly, to be just as popular with children
of the 1960s as with their parents and grandparents. The
fact that they are old-fashioned, that the speech, the clothes,
the customs are all different from those of today does not
seem to matter. They contain some essential quality which
children at once recognise as being for them. The following
list indicates the sort of book I mean. Each reader could
probably add a few and perhaps take one or two out, but
I think there would be fairly general agreement: *Treasure*

Island, Kidnapped, Masterman Ready, King Solomon's Mines, Uncle Tom's Cabin, Huckleberry Finn, What Katy Did, Little Women, Ann of Green Gables, Heidi, The Secret Garden, Black Beauty. These are books for older juniors, who, though they may still enjoy folklore will also need the more extended kind of story. One feature that all these books have in common may be noted. None of them avoids death or unhappiness. Many modern children's books take place either in an atmosphere of picnics and holidays in which there may be momentary danger, when someone is cut off by the tide, but in which unhappiness and bereavement has no place, or in an atmosphere of pure fantasy, of Batman and the Daleks. Without condemning either of these atmospheres in moderation, I would say that, since unhappiness and bereavement come to all, it may be well to meet them first in imagination and, so to speak, learn how to deal with them, and that the children's classics make this possible.

4. MODERN BOOKS. There has been, particularly since the war, a remarkable output of books for children. It is not easy for either parents or teachers to keep pace with this, even to be aware of what is available, let alone read the books. We all tend, therefore, to give to our children the books we ourselves enjoyed when we were their age. This is all right, but the modern books include many which are too good to miss. You may like to run over the following list and see how many you know or how many your children have read. All of them can be warmly recommended:

Johnny the Clockmaker (Ardizzone), *The Crotchety Crocodile* (Baumann), *Plupp builds a house* (Borg), *The Shoes Fit for a King* (Bill), *Sandy the Red Deer* (Darling), *Ching-Ting and the Ducks* (Fribourg), *Nicolette and the Mill* (Guillot), *Home on the Range* (Hadr), *Toyon* (Kalashnikoff), *The Thumbstick* (Mayne), *Children at Green Knowl* (Boston), *Pigeon Post* (Ransome), *The Hobbit* (Tolkien), *Down the Bright Stream* (B. B.), *The Man of the House* (Maclean), *The Borrowers* (Norton), *The Boy and the River* (Bosco), *The Little Prince* (St. Exupéry), *Rascal* (Sterling North), *The Flight of the Heron* (Broster). This is a very mixed list of twenty books, including some published before

1939 and some in the last decade, some suitable for sevens
and eights, some for nines and tens. The choice is so
enormous that few readers are likely to know more than half,
but if you score less than five then you may reasonably
conclude that your knowledge of children's books needs
bringing up to date! The subject matter of the twenty books
listed is very varied. It includes traditional cloak-and-sword
adventure as in *The Flight of the Heron*, fantasy as in *The
Borrowers*, modern, but pre-war, upper-class children as in
Pigeon Post, modern working-class children as in *The Man
of the House*, France as in *The Boy and the River*, America as
in *Rascal*, animals as in *Toyon* and *Rascal*, elves as in *The
Hobbit*. The list is not a miniature library for one child, but a
selection of books to suit most children.

5. POETRY. Many readers will remember having to learn
poems by heart when they were at school and then recite
them. Neither of these practices is as common as it used to be,
and since the effect of both on many children was to create in
them a hearty dislike of poetry and an unwillingness ever to
open a book of poetry again, perhaps this is a good thing. It
cannot, however, be said that any very satisfactory way of
teaching poetry has established itself, at all generally at any
rate, instead. The first requirement is a teacher who himself
understands what poetry is, knows how to read it and has
read a lot and has developed a sensitive, discriminating
taste. It is perhaps asking a good deal that there should be
such a teacher in every primary school, but without one
not much can be done. A teacher has to have the resources
to be able to choose the right poem for the right moment
and to offer as much comment (and no more) as the poem
needs.

If such teachers are rare, such parents are even rarer, and
to many, perhaps to most, it simply would not occur to give
their children poetry books, still less to read poems to them.
Yet poetry is not simply a pastime for squares. It is the
language in which emotion is most readily and, if it is good,
most controlledly expressed and, if we want to express our
emotions and at the same time keep them in order we cannot
ignore poetry. Great poetry is, for many of us, the only

means we have of knowing what great feeling is like and it is an essential part of education.

Parents who already read and enjoy poetry will need no guidance in the matter of books. They will have books of poetry in the house and will share their own loves and choices with their children. If you cannot manage this you could still put two or three books of poetry among your children's books and leave them to discover them for themselves. *Mother Goose* will supply most of what is needed for younger children, say 4–7, and then, perhaps, Geoffrey Grigson's *The Cherry Tree* (Phoenix) which contains a large number of poems with a wide and varied appeal. There are plenty of good (and bad) anthologies of poems for use in schools, but if you want a single one for the home *The Cherry Tree* is as good as any. I should also, myself, add Walter de la Mare's wonderful collection called *Come Hither* (Constable) which covers some of the same, but some very different, ground and contains the most fascinating notes which have ever been written. For a child who enjoys delving into out-of-the-way lore this book is a treasure-house.

Francis Bacon, in one of his essays, wrote: 'Reading maketh a full man' and Queen Elizabeth I, in whose reign he lived, once said: 'I pity unlearnéd gentlemen on a rainy day'. Our educational system has produced or allowed to grow up, too many 'unlearned gentlemen' who complain constantly that there is nothing to do, who, when they find something to do, do it at the expense of others, who, in fact, are not 'full men'. They have not the resources within themselves that books could give them, if they had ever formed the habit of reading them. They have learned to read, if not quite in vain, at any rate without the rewards that their effort, and that of those who taught them, deserves. The primary schools of England are trying hard to raise a better-read generation and they need the parents' help.

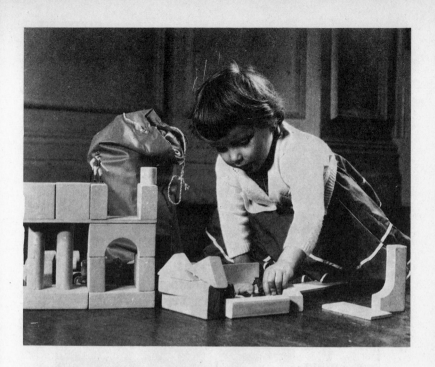

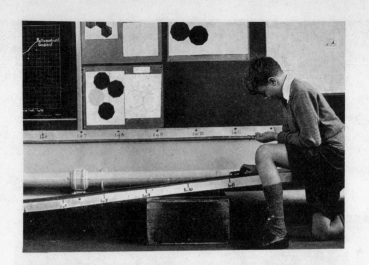

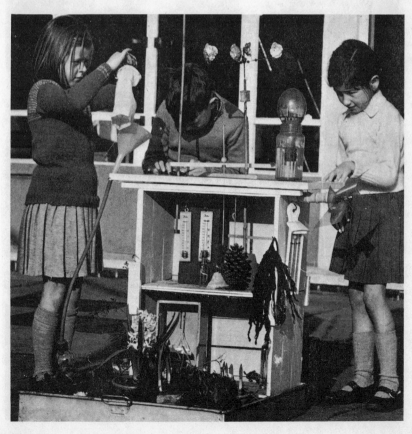

C. LEARNING TO WRITE

We have seen that children learn to speak their own language before they come to school and without any systematic teaching, and that until this has been accomplished, it is of little avail to teach them to read. Even if it is technically possible, as some educators in the U.S.A. contend, it is doubtful whether it is worth doing until the spoken language is well established as a habit and a vocabulary of possibly 6,000 words acquired. Some infants' teachers, as has been said, teach writing simultaneously with reading or even as an introduction to it. There is a good deal to be said for this. The notion of writing something of your own, something you have just said, is probably more easily assimilable at 5 than the notion of interpreting what somebody else has written down.

Thirty years ago such an idea would have seemed preposterous to almost everybody. How could children possibly write before they had learned how? The task of learning to form letters correctly, then to combine them into words and finally into sentences was a lengthy one. It involved much copying and practice, the use almost always of double-lined paper and sometimes of quadruple-lined, and was altogether a most laborious business. It was at the time rare to find any writing below the age of 8 which was not either straight copying, or dictation or an exercise. Furthermore, at about that age, just when some degree of fluency was beginning to be acquired, two brakes were applied which slowed the whole process down again. First the unjoined Roman script which had been used until then had to be abandoned and an entirely new hand, usually described as cursive and based on the copperplate handwriting of the 18th century, had to

be learned and then the admirable pencil was outlawed and
the children had to use pens. These were narrow penholders
with, usually, scratchy, spiky steel nibs which had to be
dipped in the inkpots every three words or so, often emerging
with a liquid more like mud than ink dripping from them.
I have made the worst of it, but there were too many schools
in which the conditions were exactly those.

One by one these various hindrances, masquerading as
aids, disappeared and writing in a modern infants' school is
now dealt with something as follows. The handwriting
aspect of it requires a good model from the start. Many
teachers will have a model alphabet of upper and lower
case letters permanently displayed. The styles vary according
to taste, but there is a growing tendency to use an italic
hand, that is a hand based on one of the 16th-century
styles, which is characterised by the use of a chisel-shaped
nib. The flexible steel-nib of pre-war days could only be got
to make thick strokes by the use of pressure and fine ones by
relaxing pressure, involving a use of the muscles which led
quickly to tiredness and deterioration of form. The chisel-
shaped nib makes its strokes thick or thin according to the
direction in which it is being moved and without any change
in pressure. In the opinion of many it also allows a much
more elegant, as well as a more legible, hand and, contrary
to what may be expected, it is just as speedy a hand as the
old cursive and far more able to keep its standard over
long periods of writing at speed. The teacher must of course
use the same hand as he is teaching and the children's
earliest efforts will be copies of what he has written. Even at
this first stage, however, they will not be just copies. The first
step of all is usually a picture done by the child. 'What is the
picture?' asks the teacher. 'It is a picture of my dog', replies
the child, and then either at the child's, or the teacher's
suggestion, something is written underneath it. 'What shall
we put?' asks the teacher, 'This is my dog. His name is
Peter', says the child. The teacher then writes this sentence
on a piece of paper and the child copies it. The handwriting
at this stage will be very large, done usually with a soft
pencil and may look rather crude. Practice will be needed

before a good standard is reached, but mostly practice in doing this same kind of thing, not just handwriting practice. The next stage is when the child says: 'Can I do it myself?' 'Well, try', says the teacher. The child wants to write, let us say, under a striking portrait (which would surprise the subject if she saw it!): 'This is my Mum. She is having her tea'. He gets on all right until he comes to 'having'. He may get stuck at this point and have to ask the teacher for help, or he may write 'hafing' and then 'er tee'. In the meantime he is also learning to read words and gradually he is able to manage longer sentences, to rely less on his teacher and to do without pictures. The process may be fast or slow according to the child's capacity, but it will be essentially the same in every case.

As the writing develops it will be seen to be speech in written form. This is perfectly natural and proper. Any literary quality in a six-year-old would be unusual and, though acceptable if, in an exceptional child, it is there, certainly not to be actively encouraged. The following letter sent to me by a 6-year-old boy is the kind of writing that you now find in infants' schools:

'Everyday I help my mother and we have started a Christmas play. Mrs. D—— said that you are Glad about our poem last week. We are going to see a film this afternoon. It is about Boys town in India We have brought some money to see it I gave Lewis a penny It is Gaynors Birthday to-day She is seven years old. It is nealy Christmas I am the inkeper in the play Gaynor is mary and Ian is Joseph. I wish you a merry Christmas.'

Points to be noted about this are:

1. The spelling and punctuation are exactly as in the original.
2. Out of 97 words only two 'nearly' and 'innkeeper' are spelled incorrectly.
3. It consists almost entirely of main clauses. There is only one subordinate clause.
4. There is little or no sequence. The letter simply contains all the things that the writer wished to tell me, as they came into his head.

Here is a piece by a 7-year-old child entitled "Judy and
her Doll". Again the spelling, punctuation and grammar are
unedited:

'Once up on a time there was a little girl Judy who
longed for a doll with long hair at Chrismas she wolk up
and saw a doll just as she wanted with long hair She
played with it all day then at night she put it in a shoe box
and forgot to take it upstairs with her in the morning her
mummy didn't know that her doll was in the shoe box
and gave it to the dustbinman when she woke up she
couldn't find her doll any where they were sad she ran
outside and saw her doll right on the top of the lorry she
shouted to the dustbinman she put her doll in a cot She
never lost her doll again.'

Points to be noted here are:

1. Only 'woke' and 'Christmas' are misspelt.

2. There are still few subordinate clauses compared with
main ones, in fact 3 to 15.

3. The sequence and development of the piece are a great
advance on the first.

4. The piece is interesting to read because it conveys a
personal experience.

The next piece of writing might well be thought to be by an
older child but the writer was in fact 7 years old. It is part of
a piece of composition which describes a visit to Butlin's,
containing 1,400 words and is, again, printed exactly as it was
written:

'After I had been in the Vienna Ballroom for about twelve
minutes we went into another ballroom. After we had been
in this about three minutes I saw a man with a table set
in front off him. Pinned in front off the table was a notice
that said Dr. Anthony Dare. I showed Mummy and
Daddy it and we walked over to him to see what he was
doing. When we were just opposite I looked at a pile of
papers on his desk, on the back off the papers it said if you
want your finger print rite to Doktor anthony Dare. Just
then somebody came up and asked for there finger print
Mr. Dare put some sort of blacking on their hand and
pressed it against the paper at once the paper had a black

hand on it. Anthony looked very closely at the paper and told the lady her fortune. Then he dipped some cotton wool in something on his desk. It looked like water. But I knew it was parrafin. Mr. Dare rubbed the parraffin on the lady's hand. After Mr. Dare had rubbed a lot of parraffin on the lady's hand, it soon became quite clean and the lady looked very very pleased. She paid a shilling.'

Upon this remarkable piece I would say:

1. The power of recall of detail is exceptional.

2. The number of subordinate clauses (6) in comparison with that of main clauses (21) is still small. In that respect it is typical 7-year-old writing.

3. The merit of the writing comes from the writer's passionate interest in what he saw. He had something to say.

Here is a letter from an 8-year-old of much more ordinary ability which may serve to correct the impression that I am quoting exceptional children:

'I hope you are happy. Mrs. Webb is away. She has got a very Bad cold, and we dun some sums yesterday and I got three roggng and Then we went out to play. and we play London Bridge is falling down. and Jaqueline and Doreen play. and I hope Miss Webb will soon be back I like Miss Webb and Miss Webb brotht us some berris to school and we have got some chats (charts) and They have got a picture and Miss Webb made them.

You sinserly
Marion'

There are many more mistakes in this than in either of the previous ones but it is interesting for the same reason, that it conveys a genuine personal experience. It tells us quite a lot, particularly about the teacher. It may be interesting to compare with it another letter from a boy in the same class:

'Miss Webb is away to-day and Miss Mackie is away. I am now in standard two* now, as you came to see us when we were in standard one. Mr. Brown is here for as I have told

---

* This term went on being used for the second year long after 1926 when 'standards' were abolished.

you Miss Webb is away. A bit ago we had our photographs taken they are a shilling each. Today Mr. brown
is letting us see one which is done. It is nearly my turn
now. its my turn next. I have just had my turn now. The
one in front of me has got it now. here is a secret. Captain
Beswick is coming to see us in a bit he is really a famous
explora he is coming to tell us a lot of his adventures. . .
Well goodbye and good luck.

from Bobbie.'

Here we notice the same vivid quality and some quite
dramatic hot reporting! Bobbie is clearly more able than
Marion, or was when the letters were written. Neither has
yet mastered all the conventions of writing, but each has
grasped the essentials, and is using language as an expression
of first-hand experience.

It is this insistence on the importance of subject-matter,
of having something to say that you really want to say, which
characterises the writing of children in a good primary school.
It is much better to learn to write correctly as a means of
doing this, rather than by doing artificial exercises. Some
exercises may be needed to put right recurring errors or to
fix important rules in the memory, but many teachers manage
successfully without much use of them and when they are
necessary make them up themselves instead of working
through a text-book.

The boy who wrote the following was 9 years and 10
months. He had clearly developed a keen interest in mathematics. What he had to say was not easy and we can see him
wrestling here and there with language, not always with
complete success. But that is how to learn to write!

'I have worked out how many miles in a light-year, it
is 5,847,956,000,000 miles. The nearest star is 4.3 light-
years away. When you look at the sky at night, you look
back in time. When you look at anything you look back in
history, millionths of trillionths of a second ago. That
means you never see anything at the proper time. The
sun's light takes 8 min. 20 secs. to reach us. We see the
moon approximately $1\frac{1}{4}$ secs after. If two men looked at
each other, one on a star 2,000 light-years away and one on

the earth, they would see each other 2,000 years later. So they would have wait 2000 years to see each other. So they look back through time. If a rocket could travel twice the speed of light then people could visit stars. In other words breaking the light barrier.'

This piece of writing raises another important point. Traditionally the subject-matter of English composition was drawn from common daily experience. Children wrote on 'How I help mother', 'What I do on Saturdays', 'The most exciting day of my holidays', 'Signs of spring', 'My pet', 'How to dress a doll', etc. In the modern primary school a much wider range of subject-matter is used and it is not at all exceptional to find writing about mathematics and science, history and geography, music and art.

Another new development is the writing of poetry by children. Poetry is the language of feeling and there is nothing more natural than that children should express their feelings in poetic form. Some early attempts to get them to do this ran into difficulties, because they were expected to use rhyme and metre. These involved technical difficulties which few children could grapple with and the result was usually doggerel. The struggle to find rhymes was too hard. When a freer kind of verse is encouraged, however, children take to its use very readily. What they write is seldom great poetry and is often imitative but is none the worse for that. One Headmaster deliberately tried to touch off the children's imagination by reading to them parts of T. S. Eliot's *The Waste Land*, and his wife, who was a good artist, helped by drawing some pictures which suggested the background. A ten-year-old boy, as a result, wrote the following:

'A small dirty boy stands there,
A puppet in a world of giants,
Lost in a jungle of sorrow and despair,
Trees bending, groaning mournfully,
Grass, weeds, wild plants
Eating rubble.
A deathly silence hangs over it.
The boy stands looking,
Looking at broken cycles,

At discarded toys
Wheel-less rusty cars,
Guarding the place like sentries.
A rotted wall surrounds this place of death
Leaning over the boy.
He cuts his way through.
The branches cut back
He walks away
Torn and bleeding.'

This is not a great poem but it is a kind of writing that is
worth doing and it is far from being exceptional. Most of the
poetry written *for* children is trivial, because most writers
mistakenly suppose that children are not interested, or ought
not to be interested in danger, unhappiness, loss and death.
When children write poetry themselves it is often concerned
with those very things, about which they have deep feelings.
The following poem was written by a rather backward
nine-year-old boy, in a school which served a poor, bleak
housing estate with many absentee fathers and so-called
'uncles'.

'Children sleep in their beds
While tramps use a bed of moss,
Old men get beaten by Teds
Fathers cry by their dead son's cross.
Night is the feared part of the day.'

You cannot teach children to write poetry like that, but you
can create conditions in school in which a child who has that
particular thing to say can say it. A child only writes a poem
like that for someone whom he trusts. The school in question
was a very good one indeed.

Some readers may wonder where, in all this, grammar
comes in. If a letter appears in the newspaper complaining
that children cannot write correct English the writer nearly
always asserts that the reason is that they are not taught
grammar. Sometimes he adds, showing how liberal and
reasonable he is: 'I don't of course mean formal grammar'.
Since all grammar is formal, this addition is meaningless,
and the whole controversy is based on misunderstanding.
Whatever else grammar does it does not teach children to

speak or write English correctly. Try correcting a child of
five who has said: 'We was watching the fireworks' by the use
of grammar and you will have to say: "You have used a part
of the auxiliary verb 'to be' wrongly. 'Was' is confined to the
first and third person singular. The plural is 'were' for all
three persons. The second person singular 'wast' is now
archaic". This would of course be so much gibberish to the
child and no one in their senses would try to teach that sort
of thing to an infant.

It is quite true that little boys at preparatory schools learn
Latin grammar and that some of them use it correctly, but
this is a totally different matter. Latin is a dead language which
can be reduced to clear and definite rules, and its grammar is
quite different from that of English. When you are learning
Latin the use you make of this language (writing and trans-
lating sentences) can keep pace with the grammar you have
learned. But when you are speaking your own language, you
will be using kinds of sentences and expressions which are far
beyond your knowledge of grammar.

If children in primary schools are taught grammar it is
certainly not, directly at any rate, as an aid to correctness.
Correctness, whatever that is, and it is by no means a simple
question, comes from constantly using the language for a
variety of purposes, from hearing it and reading it well used,
under careful and informed guidance. To this may be added
the study of any aspect of language which is suitable to the
age of the child. For example, the connection between sound
and sense (*onomatopoeia* or *echoism*, to use the modern term)
is something that a 9-year-old child can appreciate, while
metaphor, one of the most important and interesting features
of language, has to be postponed, for most, until the secondary school stage. Any study which leads to a greater interest
in language, a greater sensitiveness to it, a greater apprecia-
tion of its possibilities, will contribute to its better use, and
such studies may include material which would normally
be classified as grammar. But we must be careful of state-
ments like: 'well surely they ought to know the parts of
speech!' Many readers who have found the present para-
graph easy to read and who could perfectly well have written

it themselves, might pull very long faces if they were asked
to parse it, i.e. say what part of speech every word is. It is
easy enough to learn the definition of a noun, a verb, an
adjective, etc. and this may be worth doing, but it is much
harder to spot the part of speech in use. So many words in
English can be used as two or even three different parts.
It is no use saying: " 'Before' is a preposition, for it is also an
adverb and a conjunction". It is no use saying " 'Side' is a
noun, for it can also be used as an adjective (side street, side
issue) and, as a verb (side the table, side with someone)".
This in itself is interesting, but for young children it may be
confusing. Whether they learn it or not will, however, have no
effect on whether they use 'before' and 'side' correctly. They
could do that before they came to school at all!

I have written at some length about grammar because,
like multiplication tables, it is something that often worries
parents. 'She doesn't even know what a verb is!' they say, or
'When I was his age I knew all the parts of speech', and they
feel that their children are not being properly taught. If the
children are going to learn a foreign language the alarm is
heightened, and to make matters worse they hear it said
that the teachers in the grammar school complain bitterly
that the children 'don't know any grammar'. Having taught
both French and Latin in a grammar school myself, I know
that this is a very ill-founded complaint. The grammar of
English, as I have said, is very different from that of Latin
and of French, and the grammar of the latter is much better
learned *with* the language itself. To take a single example, the
object. In Latin the object must be put into the accusative
case if it is direct, into the dative if it is indirect, and that
means altering the end of the word (inflection). In French the
object, if it is a pronoun, must precede the verb, unless the
verb is imperative, and if it is direct the past participle in a
compound tense must agree with it. These are essential pieces
of knowledge for the correct use of Latin and French, but the
whole of the last two sentences is totally irrelevant to English,
in which the object is recognised simply by its position in
the sentence and there are no inflections and no concords
involved in its relation to the verb. Most teachers of languages

in secondary schools now realise that it is much quicker and better to learn the grammar of the language with it, and are well satisfied if children come to them from the primary school able to use English well and with their interest in language already aroused.

D. SPEECH AND CONVERSATION

We have seen how, in its essentials, speech is learned between
the ages of one and four and that children arrive in school
with that great learning feat behind them. There are two
questions which arise at the next stage. First, how is this
habit of speech developed in school? and secondly, What is or
ought to be done to teach children to speak 'correctly'?

If you go into a primary school today you may be surprised
to find how much talking goes on. It was once the mark of a
good teacher that he could 'keep his class quiet', and some
readers may recall a teacher of the old *régime* in whose class
nobody dared to speak unless he told them to. 'When he
op'd his lips, no dog barked.' Such readers might be shocked
at finding a hum of conversation going on without the
teacher apparently doing anything about it. Is this simply a
sign of increasingly slack discipline or does it make sense
educationally?

It must be said at once that there *is* a kind of noise which
does indicate exasperation, or resentment or boredom in a
class and that this is an almost total obstacle to learning. It
means that, for whatever reason, inexperience, incompetence,
infirmity or lack of sympathy, the teacher has failed to gain
the co-operation of the children. The symptoms are
unmistakeable and any experienced teacher will recognise
them instantly. The hum of conversation in a good primary
class is something quite different. It is not natural for young
children either to sit still or to remain silent for more than a
very short time. They have to learn to do both as they grow
older, but this will not happen by making them do either
before they are ready for it. Besides, one of the ways in which
things are understood and learned is through discussion.

'Let's see what we feel when we've had a talk about it', we say, and thus show that we often cannot understand something until we have tried to put it into words. And in the course of discussion we learn a lot, not only about the things being discussed, but about how to compare notes, how to disagree, how to argue, how to weigh up arguments, when to ask a third party to come in and help and so on. It is all this which is going on in the primary school classroom. The children are learning through discussion among themselves.

There is no guarantee that all the conversation is relevant. Two boys who are supposed to be constructing an electric motor may in fact be talking about last Saturday's football match. There was equally no guarantee, under the old *régime*, that all the children were attending. Some only looked as if they were, and took the risk of being caught out by an unexpected question. But if there is no guarantee in the new methods, there is plenty to make waste of time unlikely. First the teacher will be moving about among the class, joining in, overhearing, watching and, secondly, the children will understand why they are doing what they are doing. If it is interesting and absorbing, worth doing in fact, they will need no explanation. If it is difficult or even boring they will have been told why they must do it, and the interval between the means and the attainment will be suited to their years. Primary children cannot think very far ahead. It is no use telling them that they will be glad when they are older that they have learned something. The satisfaction can be postponed for a little while but not for long. Meanwhile the conversation flows, though the experienced teacher, when he wants silence and attention because it is needed, will get it.

The question of 'correct' speech is not an easy one. To begin with it is very difficult to say what it is, in terms either of pronunciation, or vocabulary or even grammar. Is it 'correct' to say 'ahfternoon' 'ăfternoon' or 'uffternoon'? Not all readers will agree. Is it 'correct' to say 'moidered' or 'mythered'? Does 'starved' mean 'hungry' or 'cold'? It depends on what part of England you are in. Do you say, 'I resent you saying that' or 'I resent your saying that'? The second is grammatical but most people would say the first. The fact is that there is no such thing as correct English, there is only the English that people use. Some of their usages are purely local. Some are associated with social class (it is 'upper class' to say 'an 'otel' instead of 'a hotel', it is common to say 'shut yer trap'). Some are genteel ('perspire' for 'sweat', 'toilet' for 'W.C.'). But it is almost entirely a matter of personal opinion as to what is 'correct'. Most people are probably satisfied with the way they speak and some are hostile to anything different, calling it 'vulgar' or 'snobbish' as the case may be. Most people who change their social and economic background change their speech to suit, especially when they move 'up' in the social scale. There are exceptions to this. The late Mr. George Tomlinson, when he was Minister of Education, spoke pretty broad Lancashire and dropped his aitches. The present Prime Minister, though his speech is recognisably Yorkshire, speaks a much more upper-class kind of English.

In all this welter what is the poor teacher to do? First he tries to help the children to speak clearly. Whatever accent or vocabulary they use, if they do not speak clearly they will not be understood. Even this is not as simple as it sounds, because what sounds very un-clear to the teacher may be perfectly well understood by the child's parents and friends. Nevertheless good articulation is a useful and, in many cases, an essential piece of learning, and the teacher is justified in trying to get it. *How* he gets it is another matter. It was common, just before the war, to see 'speech-training' on an elementary school time-table. This usually consisted of rhymes, exercises and tongue-twisters designed to give practice in correct vowel-sounds. (How now brown cow, Cool blue pools), clear end-consonants (I thought that I caught the first notes of the Great Tit) and so on. These were very artificial and their final effect was small. The vowel-sounds and the end-consonants continued much as before.

The modern view is that plenty of opportunity for conversation, the speaking of poetry and drama and reading aloud, under the continuous care of the teacher and with the teacher's example before them will bring about the gradual improvement of speech in a natural way. There is undoubtedly a great deal in this argument, but it is open to question whether something more might not be done. When members of the public are interviewed on television their performance is too often appallingly bad and, on the whole, the young are worse than the old. There are other nations which seem to do much better. I would therefore say that speech-training for children is something that needs more research and experiment. In the meantime parents must remember that it is they from whom their children learn to speak and not be too ready to blame the schools if the results are not satisfactory!

CHAPTER SEVEN

Mathematics

The changes that are taking place in the teaching of mathematics in primary schools began only very recently. Ten years ago a middle-aged visitor would have found things much as they were when he was at school himself, but now he would certainly be surprised, and might be bewildered, by what he found in an increasing number of schools. At first sight this may seem to be very odd. There are no new discoveries in elementary mathematics. The relationships between the numbers remain what they always have been and there might seem to be little or no room for innovation. What has happened to bring about such a big change? Why was change thought necessary? What is mathematics now like in a modern primary school?

Before trying to answer these questions it may be useful to ask another. Why teach mathematics at all? It would be interesting to know what immediate answers to the last question spring to the reader's mind. Is mathematics useful? If we think of the amount of the mathematics learned at school that most of us use in our ordinary lives we may be surprised at how small it is. A little counting, getting and giving the right change, doing our personal accounts, using a tape measure, a calendar and a clock—that is about all. L.C.M.s and H.C.F.s, vulgar fractions, apart from halves and quarters, decimals (until 1970), area, volume, algebra, geometry—all the hours at school spent on those were wasted if we judge their value by the use we make of what we learned. If we are teachers, or chemists, or physicists or engineers or computer-programmers we may be using mathematics all the time, but the great majority use it very little. On grounds of utility the claims of mathematics are not very strong. Only a very small amount is necessary.

Another reason advanced for teaching mathematics is that it is a training in accuracy and exactness which carries over into all departments of life. This is a cherished belief, still held by many people, but there is little or no evidence to support it. The accuracy that you may learn from doing mathematics is mathematical accuracy, but you may remain just as inaccurate as ever in your other thinking or in your use of English.

The real reason for learning mathematics is that it is part of man's cultural heritage and is, or can be, tremendously interesting and exciting. To deprive children of it is as bad as to deprive them of poetry or art or music. To quote from *Primary Education* (1959), the D.E.S.'s handbook for teachers: 'Mathematical thought is part, and a great part, of the heritage of the race. . . . By its aid man has measured the distances to the stars, forecast eclipses, navigated the seas and air, made maps of the earth, built cathedrals and bridges, split atoms and designed machines from the simple lever to the most complicated space satellite or electronic computer; all the elaborate business transactions between men, between groups of men and between nations are founded on a knowledge of mathematics.' Few of us, of course, do any of these things ourselves, but they are all of general importance to every one of us and, in fact, no one has ever seriously suggested the omission of mathematics from the school curriculum. How many readers, however, found mathematics 'tremendously interesting and exciting' when they were at school and how many thought it 'difficult and wearisome'? How many, it may be wondered, could still do half the things they were taught at school and how many would have a dread feeling of panic if suddenly asked any but the most simple and straightforward mathematical question. 'How many feet in a third of a mile?' Time yourself in giving the answer! Or, a little more difficult, 'If the hands of a clock are exactly together every 65 minutes, is the clock fast, slow or keeping the right time?' How long did that take you?

It was high time to take a new look at primary mathematics. Readers who have a taste for mathematics, who are 'good at it' if you like, would find it worth while to read the *School Council's Bulletin No.* 1 (1965) entitled *Mathematics in Primary Schools* (H.M.S.O.), a fascinating, illustrated pamphlet which describes in detail the principles and the practices involved. This chapter is written for those who, for one reason or another, do not wish to pursue the matter to any depth, but who are puzzled by what they hear. It is disconcerting when your child asks for help in some mathematical homework to find that you are quite unable to understand it or to have your well-meant attempts to help swept aside with an impatient: 'Oh *that*'s not how we do it'.

We must begin by recalling what was said in Chapter 2. It will be remembered that children learn by stages and that it is no use hurrying them on to later stages before they have mastered earlier ones. Piaget (see p. 27) devoted much time and trouble to investigating how children learn mathematics and, in particular, the concepts known as 'Conservation' and 'Reversal'. 'Conservation' is the fact that if you start with a given number of objects or a given quantity of material, e.g. liquid, the quantity remains the same however you arrange it or divide it up. 'Reversal' is the fact that if you reverse a process you return to the state of affairs from which you started, e.g. you have ten pennies, you take away five and there are five left. You add five and once again you have ten. These are so obvious to us that we may wonder what the fuss is about, but they are not obvious to young children, as Piaget discovered.[14] He found for example that, if a quantity of liquid in a broad low jug is poured into a narrow high jug, children of up to about six will think that the quantity has increased because the level is higher and that no amount of teaching will affect this. The experiments were numerous, and carefully planned and conducted, and they enabled Piaget to define, with considerable clarity, the various stages in this process. Teachers would be much more hesitant than he was in assigning the stages to particular ages. We have seen (Chapter 1) how unreliable chronological age is as a criterion. But the sequence and characteristics of the stages themselves are almost universally accepted.

If it is no use teaching something before the child is ready for it and if, even when faced with the concrete situation, i.e. the two jugs and the liquid, the child still does not grasp this, to us, self-evident fact, what is to be done? The answer is that the child must discover the fact for himself in his own time. He will do this if the relevant material is available to him in sufficient quantity and variety, if he is given many opportunities of handling it and trying it out (playing with it if you like) and if his teacher is constantly on the watch to assist the passage from one stage to the next, to encourage the dawn of understanding, to detect it when it happens and to open the way ahead. This will involve constant participation by the teacher and much discussion with the children, and by the children among themselves. The importance of this was early realised by Piaget and it has been reinforced by later research. Children have been shown to make better progress *mathematically* if the mathematical experience is accompanied by appropriate language. The old arithmetic lesson, a short introductory explanation followed by ten sums worked in silence,was not only dull. It was thoroughly ineffective as a means of learning mathematics.

This brief account of the principles involved may help to explain what the visitor will find in a modern primary school. He will find the children working individually or in groups. He will find them doing different things. He will find them handling material, not just doing sums, and he will hear a great deal of conversation going on. He will also find them practising things that they already understand, because experience has shown that this is necessary. The practice *follows* the discovery. In the old days it was the other way round. Children were taught the process first, they practised it and sometimes never came to the discovery at all, but simply performed the process mechanically in the way they had been taught. It was only necessary to disguise it a little or wrap it up in a problem to discover how few really understood it. Readers may like to do the sum $\frac{3}{4} \div \frac{1}{2}$ and then explain to their own satisfaction why the answer is what it is. If they have been taught division of fractions in a mechanical way, they may well find this difficult!

Teachers, if they are to found their work on the principles described and not on the contents of a text-book, have to know what, in general, are the mathematical concepts, processes and facts which it is profitable to teach to their children. By the time he is 7 the *average* child can cope with the following, for which I have used the summary given in *Mathematics in the Primary School* (p. 11) somewhat adapted for the non-mathematical reader:

1. Sorting and classifying objects into sets. Comparing sizes of two sets (i.e. the number of objects in each) by matching; learning the language of inequality (e.g. more than, smaller than, etc.) and later the symbols ($>$ and $<$).

2. Counting the number of objects in a set. Conservation of numbers. Composition of numbers up to 20 (i.e. how they are made up of smaller numbers, e.g. 6 is $5 + 1$, $4 + 2$, $3 + 3$, $3 + 2 + 1$) without counting on or counting back (i.e. knowing that $16 + 4 = 20$, without having to count on from 16, whether the fingers are used or not).

3. The number line, that is numbers in order, up to 100, but, except for a few children, no written manipulation of numbers beyond 20. The understanding of place-value in number notation, e.g. understanding that the value of each of the three 2s in 222 depends upon the place it occupies, is gradually dawning at this stage, but it is not usually firmly established. It only reached England in the 12th century![15]

4. Measurement, i.e. knowing how to use a ruler and other simple instruments of measurement. Money, i.e. the small amounts of daily life. Conservation of measures. Knowledge of the relationships between one unit and another (e.g. pence and shillings, inches and feet, ounces and pounds, pints and quarts, i.e. the common units which are within young children's experience).

5. Simple fractions; halves, quarters, three-quarters.

6. Shape and size, including some simple proportion, e.g. 'twice as big' 'three times as long' 'half as old'.

7. Such aspects of addition, subtraction, multiplication and division as arise in the classroom.

It may be as well to emphasise once again that some children will be able to cope with considerably more than this when they are seven and some with considerably less and that the worst possible thing for any parent to do is to try to hurry the child on ahead of his understanding.

It would take too long to show how each of these aspects is dealt with in the classroom. For that I must refer the reader again to *Mathematics in the Primary School*. Here, I shall give, first of all, a short selected list of some of the things done, using the same seven subdivisions of the summary and then describe in detail one or two examples of work with slightly older children:

1. Sorting different objects in a shop, bananas, apples, cakes, etc. Laying a table with the right number of knives for the people and the same number of forks. Arranging things in order, e.g. one pea, two beans, three nuts, four apples, five oranges.

2. Counting all sorts of different objects and writing the number down (this is much better than patterns of dots and dominoes which are static). Weighing in scales to answer such questions as 'How many acorns balance 5 conkers?'

The shop again is useful. Setting out the stock (so many of each article), fixing different price labels, selling the articles, counting the takings, counting the remaining stock, entering it in a stock book, showing the number needed to bring the stock up to the original figure.

3. The number line, or number track as it is often called, is what it sounds like, a long strip of graph paper 1 inch wide and 100 ins. long, numbered 1 to 100 with the 10s marked in some prominent way. This is fixed to the wall horizontally and strips of differing sizes from 1 inch to 10 inches are prepared, which are used to find the answer to various number combinations or how far it is from one point to another.

4. There are enormous numbers of ways in which measurement may be learned, some incidental, some with a definite purpose. Measuring the classroom and its parts,

measuring the playground, measuring the children, their height, weight, girth and span and so on, measuring curves, guessing followed by measuring, measuring with one unit, and with two, and in every case discovering by discussion, trial and error how to do it, are all within the compass of an infants' school.

5. Simple fractions are very easily managed by infants and they understand the expressions 'half', 'quarter', 'three-quarters' long before the symbols $\frac{1}{2}$, $\frac{1}{4}$, and $\frac{3}{4}$ to which they are not introduced until they have had a lot of concrete experience of dividing things up into the fractions and remainders concerned.

6. Shapes are of great fascination to children and the patterns of tiles, or woodblocks on floors and of many wallpapers and fabrics will be scrutinised with interest and can be used as an introduction. Cardboard boxes can be cut so as to form a flat shape and then built up again, in the course of which the children begin to grasp the connection between a cube and its 'net'. This is the beginning of much more advanced mathematical work which, until recently, would have had no place in primary schools at all, because it would have been introduced by formulas and called 'solid' geometry.

7. The essential point is that the operations of addition, subtraction, multiplication and division should be performed not at first through symbols but on real materials. Before $3 \times 4 = 12$ is learned, three sets of four must be handled and the four sets of three, in a number of different materials or objects. It must be realised that three sets of four oranges make twelve oranges, but also that four oranges and four apples and four bananas make twelve pieces of fruit, just as three oranges, three apples, three bananas and three pears make twelve pieces. Not until this sort of ground has been very thoroughly explored should the symbols $+$, $-$, $\times$ and $\div$ be introduced, and they should at once be given their proper names, plus, minus, multiply and divide.

Children who receive this kind of foundation of mathematical experience and knowledge in the infants' school can proceed with confidence and ever-widening interest and capacity through the later stages. They extend their number-knowledge, so that they are thoroughly at home with the first 100 numbers and can manipulate them in all sorts of ways. They know their multiplication and division tables, not as something to be chanted in a sing-song voice without understanding. They really understand place-value and they can proceed to the use of other bases than 10, particularly the binary (2) base which is now of such importance since it must be used for all electronic computer work. Older people, brought up on only the denary (10) base, often find it very difficult to handle binary arithmetic. Children find no such difficulty.

In the junior school, measurement develops with the use of calculations as well as of instruments. The height of church spires, the breadth of rivers can be calculated, and this will often be done in the field, not as sums about imaginary spires and streams but with real ones. Averages, ratio, proportion and rate are introduced and simple statistics. At many points the children will use graphs. There is a delightful description in *Mathematics in Primary Schools* (p. 78) of some 10-year-olds who had become interested in the relation between the number of sides of a regular shape and the size of its angles. This had happened, incidentally, when their teacher was ill, so they had to organise themselves. The following is an account of what they did: 'We drew the graph . . . up to twelve sides. The graph turned out to be a curve so Michael and I decided to see if there was a turning point. The graph was of extra interest because if we could reach 180° we should have come to a figure supposedly made by a straight line. We continued the graph to 240 sides and then discontinued it because it looked as though it would go on for ever'. (The children then turned their attention to the figure pattern.) 'We jumped in 10s, 50s, 100s, 1,000s and finally 1,000,000 in our efforts to reach 180°. When we saw the pattern we realised we should never reach 180° or turn the graph. On May 11th at 10.15 a.m. we finally gave in. We think this is the most exciting piece of mathematics we have ever done. It is just like research work.'

This little account is worth reflection for a number of reasons. It is a good, clear, expressive piece of English. The actual arithmetic involved is very simple, but it needed accuracy and patience and so did the graph. Such obviously intelligent children might have been expected to know the answer in advance, namely that no figure can be enclosed by a straight line. The writing shows that they did know this but they wanted to prove it mathematically. In order to do this they took immense trouble, and the conclusion of the account makes it clear that the experience was worth having and, since their teacher was not there, self-motivated. The account provides much information about the modern primary school. The pace and breadth of learning, compared with that of the old elementary school, is terrific.

Another piece of work done by some 9-and 10-year-olds will now be described. They were given five irregularly shaped pieces of stone and asked to find out the relationship between their volume and their weight. The easiest part of the problem was to find and record the weight of each stone. The children had had a good deal of experience in solving problems of this kind and they used a calibrated glass container with water in it to find out the volume of each stone by the volume of water it displaced. This gave them two sets of figures. They were accustomed to using graphs and they therefore made a graph with weight on one axis and volume on the other and plotted the results of their measuring. They noticed that the graph was a straight line except for one kink, from which they concluded that they had made a mistake. They checked their measurements but the kink was still there so they suspected that the stone which caused the kink was in some way different from the others. This was how they first met with density, not as a theoretical concept in a secondary school text-book, but as an observable fact.

It is worth while noticing what all this involved. It required great accuracy in weighing the stones, in measuring the amount of water displaced and in plotting the graph. It required constructive thought. There was nothing ready-made about the problem. It contained a self-correcting element, the kink, which led to a new discovery, that solid objects have not only weight and volume but also density. It required careful planning by the teacher who had to see that the right materials were available. The lack of a calibrated glass container, for example, would have introduced a further difficulty which might have proved too much for the children.

Any reader who feels an inclination to say that all this is 'just playing about' may like to try this little problem himself, and he will soon gain a new respect for children, for their teachers and for the new mathematics! As someone who had been watching children at this kind of work once remarked: 'If we aren't careful we shall have them educated!'

CHAPTER EIGHT

Exploring the world

A one-year-old child shows insatiable curiosity. He touches everything he can reach. He pulls books out of cases. He knocks things over. He picks up whatever he finds and often tries to eat it. This is his way of finding out what the physical world is like. Later, when he can use words, he asks questions. If his parents encourage this and try to answer what he asks, his curiosity and desire to learn will grow. If they don't listen, or refuse to answer, or tell him to shut up, his desire to learn may wilt and perhaps become destructive. The foundation is laid by the parents whether they do it well or badly and by the time the child gets to school the good or the damage is done. The school can build on the good but it cannot repair the damage, or only to a limited extent. The essential job is the parent's and not the teacher's.

This desire to find out, to explore the world, if it is nurtured from the start, is the most powerful force in education and it can last for a lifetime, although, as we saw in Chapter 2, it usually declines as life advances. The knowledge of the world that man has now acquired is stupendous and so is the amount of which he is still ignorant. It is convenient, and necessary, for many purposes to classify the knowledge and call some of it history, some geography, some science, and so on. These classifications themselves have to be divided up into more specialised classes, economic history, political history, the history of engineering, physical geography, human geography, meteorology for example. Science is divided into innumerable specialised sciences, nuclear physics, physical chemistry, organic chemistry, ornithology, plant biology, etc., etc., which are always tending to subdivide even further as knowledge grows and it becomes impossible for any one man to know more than a small section.

Many of these subdivisions have very little meaning for most of us. We manage quite well with the single word physics and seldom use or understand terms such as nuclear physics, bio-physics, astro-physics, soil physics, etc. We leave this to the experts. There is not much else we can do. For primary children even the broader subdivisions of knowledge have little meaning. They are interested and they want to know, but their curiosity and their questions will cross the boundaries of subject from minute to minute. A boy who is looking at a limestone church and asks where the stone came from, or what the odd little squiggles in it are, or how it was cut will not be told: 'We are doing history now, not geography, or geology or technology'. Forty years ago, when history was simply a class lesson assisted by a text-book, the questions would not have been asked or if they had been might well have been squashed. Once children come up against the real thing, however, this kind of compartmenting of knowledge becomes impossible.

I want to illustrate this by returning to a school that I have already mentioned in Chapter 6 (page 62). It may be remembered that the children and the headmaster had excavated the site of the mediaeval village which was in a meadow adjacent to the school. This was a spare-time activity undertaken after school on summer evenings, but it provided a great deal of material which was used in school. The foundations that were uncovered had to be accurately measured and plans drawn of them. Objects had to be identified and described or drawn whether they were tools, or implements, or human or animal remains. No one could say, at any given moment, whether they were doing mathematics, English, art, history or biology, but they were certainly learning and finding out how to classify.

When the dig was finished the whole proceedings were warmly praised by the Department of Works which had, initially, been rather alarmed at hearing that a mediaeval site was being 'dug up by a lot of kids'. The soil was replaced and the turf restored, but the children were not content to go

back to the old routine, nor did their headmaster intend
that they should. There were plenty of other things to discover in their village. They made a map of all the birds'
nests they could find within 100 yards of the school, identified
the species and kept a watch to see how many eggs were laid
in each and what proportion of fledglings survived. This
needed much care, patience and self-control, much accurate
recording, much use of books. A further interest which
developed from the excavation was the making of a collection of skulls, from a cow's to a fieldmouse's. They wanted to
find some means of measuring the brain cavities of each
and so comparing the sizes in a significant way. They hit
upon the idea of sealing the cavities with plasticine and then
filling them with dry sand. To measure the quantity of sand
they constructed, out of drawing paper, containers with a
volume of one cubic inch. These did very well for the larger
skulls but were too big for measuring the smaller ones
accurately, so they constructed a container the sides of which
measured half an inch. They soon discovered, to their
surprise, that this container when full held not half the
amount of sand as the other, but an eighth. They were not
likely ever to forget the relationship of volume to area,
something that many grown-up people have to think twice
about before they get it right.

When I visited this school I was invited, within a minute
or two of arriving, by one of the 10-year-old boys to have a
look at what he was doing. In the middle of showing me, he
suddenly remarked: 'The trouble here is that we haven't
enough time to do what we want. We are trying to get the
headmaster to start a night school for us so that we can get on
with our work in the evening'.* It is perhaps worth adding
that, judged even by the most conventional standards of
neatness, accuracy and correctness, this school came out very
well.

Two objections may be made to this way of treating the
subject-matter of science, history and geography. First,
there is the possibility that the children, though admittedly

* This story is told in the Plowden Report, Vol. 1, p. 268.

interested, will learn odds and ends and that their knowledge will not hang together. The second is that the subjects of science, history and geography will be so haphazardly and incompletely covered that there will be no foundation on which the secondary schools can build.

The first thing to be said about these objections is that the possible subject-matter of science, history and geography is so vast that, whatever plan is followed, only a tiny portion can be covered. All schemes of work are selective. The ages and capacities of the children have to be taken into account and then the teacher must decide (or let the writer of a text-book decide for him) what is to be included and what left out. There is no basic agreed minimum and there could not be. Secondly, a teacher who works on the system described above will, if he knows his business, keep a very careful record of work done and, so arrange matters, that the children receive a balanced education and cover a reasonable amount of ground. Thirdly, though many teachers use the method some of the time, few, except in infants' schools, use it all the time, and many still keep the subjects partly separate. The connections between them are obvious and most teachers make good use of them. History and geography, science and mathematics, geography and science, history and music, with English having a vital role at every point, are clearly closely connected, but the amount of dovetailing and integration that is used will vary from school to school and from class to class. In the sections that follow I shall discuss science, history and geography as separate subjects but in a way which will show how they are connected in themselves and in the classroom.

Until quite recently the only science taught in primary schools was natural history or 'nature study' as it was always called on the time-tables. This consisted of lessons on such topics as 'The spring awakening', 'summer visitors', 'seeds and their dispersal', 'Preparing for Winter'. The children were encouraged to bring specimens—berries, wild flowers, leaves, shells, caterpillars, etc.—and in many schools some attempt was made to keep live creatures in the classroom, goldfish, tadpoles and caterpillars being the favourites, with mice and hamsters as runners-up. This was all right as far as it went. Living things are always of interest to children who enjoy collecting them and caring for them. Even schools in the middle of towns were able to do something on these lines by visiting neighbouring parks, waste spaces such as the 'crofts' of Lancashire towns and, from time to time, the open country on the outskirts of the town or even further afield.

At its best this was and is very good. The children learn a little of how life is lived, they learn to observe and to think about what they see, they learn to use books of reference and how to record what they find. There is some good observation as well as evident delight in the following by a 9-year-old boy:

'Over there I have just seen a little skylark rise from the ground. There he goes, straight up into the blue sky, singing as he goes and the higher he rises the louder his song seems to become. He has got such a lovely quivering voice, not quite like any other bird.

'Mrs. Skylark makes her nest on the ground in the grass and she likes to choose a little hollow, it might be one made by a horses hoof and this she lines with grass; Mother and father skylark both sing, and they look very much alike in their speckled brown feathers. Their eggs are a pale greyish couler and covered with brown spots. I often wonder how they manage to hatch out at all when I think how exposed to danger they are.'

The recent changes in science teaching have not expelled natural history from the curriculum or only when it was so badly done that it was no loss. What has happened is that a lot of other science has been added. There were several good reasons for doing this. Important as biology is, a scientific education which is confined to it, is very lopsided. Children are interested in all sorts of things which would come under the headings of electricity, magnetism, optics, mechanics and chemistry, and to leave them out of the primary school curriculum is to throw away good means of education. Finally some teachers are much more at home in the physical sciences than in the natural ones and will teach better if they can include some of the former in their syllabus.

The aim of teaching science in a primary school is not really to lay the foundations of scientific knowledge, still less to offer elementary introductions to different sciences. It is to use the things that interest children—electric motors, pulleys, magnets, levers, magnifying glasses, lenses, model railways, pumps, pendulums, water-wheels, windmills, elastic, wire, string, telephones, thermometers, barometers, compasses, etc., etc.—as means of education. They find out not only how they work, but what questions it is sensible to ask about them and how to find the answers and check their accuracy. A lot of the apparatus that they use will be home-made and so much the better. Some children who were asked the question: 'How strong is string?' had to think out ways of answering it and procure the apparatus they needed. They had to choose different samples of string and then subject each sample to the same series of tests, by attaching weights and noting at what point the string broke. The tests had to be repeated for checking and the samples finally arranged in order of strength with breaking-weight attached. What was the use of this you may ask? It had not perhaps much practical use. Certainly it did not help very much in choosing a string for tying up a Christmas parcel. But it was a simple way of introducing children to the techniques of testing, a first step in scientific thinking and one they found interesting and within their power, not merely to understand, but to perform.

It would be necessary to give many examples in order to show all the possibilities of this kind of learning. One more must do. The apparatus was an inexpensive Gauge O oval track clockwork model railway, the sort of thing that children are given and play with before the real model railway fever develops and that they then reject in favour of Gauge OO, scale models and 'real' track. In this case the play was turned to good account. Every boy knows that the engine will go round faster without any trucks than with some. The question was 'How much faster?' These children had no stop-watch and had to do the best they could with the second hand of a wristwatch. The engine was timed five times for a simple circuit, then a truck was added and the timing was repeated, then a second truck and so on until all four trucks, which was all they had, were on the train. The trucks were weighed and a graph was drawn showing the relationship of speed to weight of load. But the children noticed that, if the engine was allowed to run its full wind, not only did the train slow down towards the end of the wind but it stopped after covering a shorter distance as each new truck was added. So there was a weight-distance ratio as well as a weight-speed ratio. What was the connection between them? Quite a lot of scientific enquiry was opened up by that toy railway.

It will not have escaped your notice that the experiment with the stones described in Chapter 7 might equally well have been included here and the experiment with the model railway put into Chapter 7. The learning of science has always required some mathematical knowledge and ability. What is new is that, at this early stage in the primary school, the two are learned in conjunction and, so to speak, help each other. 'Scientific method is a device for forcing a new way of seeing'.16 This is true at the advanced stage of which the writer was speaking, but it is also true at the primary stage and these two examples, I think, illustrate it very clearly.

Science is fashionable and for very good reasons, so that no excuse is required for including it in the curriculum. Geography and History, time-honoured school subjects though they are, are rather less secure, especially perhaps History.

'history is about chaps,
geography is about maps'
but of course geography is 'about chaps' too and indeed about almost everything else. A study of geography will involve not only the stock geographical subject-matter, land forms, rivers, seas and so on, but also vegetation, climate, weather, costume, religion, race, food, drink, building materials, design of buildings, customs and habits, economics, history, politics, to name only some of the topics, which sooner or later are forced on the geographer's attention.

In primary schools, the geography may include some study of the neighbourhood, some knowledge of the British Isles and some of one or more foreign countries. There will, of course, be books and maps, pictures and photographs, perhaps a projector and a television set. The children of today have far better opportunities than their grandparents had for knowing what other parts of the world and their inhabitants look like. You will find collections of stamps and of labels of foreign goods, especially fruit, displayed on the walls and there may be a link between the school and some other school overseas. Sometimes there will be examples of foreign crafts and posters and notices in foreign languages. All these provide a good background and are certainly worth having but they are only a background or at best, material, to assist study. The study is more likely to consist of a rather detailed look at some particular place or occupation or aspect of life than of a list of facts to be learned. Facts of course are important but they must mean something to those who learn them. It is only of very slight use to know that the Nile, the Niger, the Zambesi and the Orange River are all in Africa if you have no notion of the differences between life on any of them.

The geography of the British Isles is handled in much the same way, with plenty of illustrative material, and emphasis on sharply differing areas—the South Yorkshire coalfields, the Worcestershire orchards, the East Anglian wheat-lands, the northern hills, the rich south-western pastures, the industrial midlands and so on.

Except that much more visual material is now available and in use, geography, as so far described, is not dramatically different from what it was in primary schools thirty years ago. There has been however a great development in local studies in which, naturally, geographical subject-matter has an important place. The ideas behind this are very simple, namely that children learn more readily from first-hand experience, i.e. from what they can touch and see, that the neighbourhood of the school can be looked at as a whole in which geography, history and almost everything else are comprised, and that it will be easier for the children to understand what they are told about other countries if they have studied at first hand the corresponding features of their own.

One school in Oxfordshire undertook such a local study. They were very fortunately placed, on the great limestone escarpment which runs from south-west to north-east across the heart of England, with the lovely valley of the Windrush at their door. It was this valley that they took as their study. At different times they traced it from its source at Teddington in Worcestershire to its junction with the Thames near Standlake. They followed it through the quiet uplands to Bourton-on-the-Water, southwards to the village which has taken its name from the stream, down through Great Barrington and Taynton to the incomparable Burford, through the meads to Minster Lovell, where beautiful ruins are all that remain of a once famous palace, and so through Witney to the Thames. How much they learned about rivers and valleys in general and about this one in particular, about the vegetation and the wild-life that they support, about the nature of limestone, about churches and houses, about the wool-trade and its wealth, about the England of Plantagenet, Tudor, Stuart and Hanoverian, could only be appreciated by one who had seen what they had written and drawn, and heard them talk about what they had seen. This was real learning in which geography, history and science were intermixed and a sense of beauty and even perhaps reverence was experienced.

But we cannot all live in the Windrush valley. I can think of another school in the blackest, most uninspiring quarter of an industrial city in Lancashire, surrounded apparently by rows of back-to-back houses. This school also did a local study. They took the square half-mile in which the school stood and went through it with a toothcomb. They found out the occupations of all the inhabitants, fortunately perhaps a most respectable body of people, they visited the six shops in the area and made a map of the world showing where all the imported goods came from. They visited and found out all they could about the Victorian gothic church. They visited a coalmine that came within the area. They discovered, to everybody's surprise, a small area of cultivated ground and made crop plans based on the information given to them by the owner. Finally they decided to explore the sewage system. This was vetoed, but it led to a visit from an official who explained to them how it worked. All this was charted and written up. They did not perhaps discover much beauty, but they learned something of social history and organisation and something of how to study and to gather information.

Teachers have to keep a careful eye on this sort of thing, to make sure that the children do not make unreasonable requests or intrude where they are not wanted. Carefully planned, it can provide, on top of everything else, a training in courtesy and good manners, in learning how to ask and how to say 'thank-you'.

You will have noticed how history crept in to a section in which I was supposed to be writing about geography. About history, considered separately as a subject, it is particularly difficult to generalise. Some teachers have gone as far as to say that it is not a primary school subject at all, because it is concerned with the behaviour of grown-up people, which is beyond the understanding of young children. If by history is meant political history, then most of us would probably agree. The causes of the Civil War, for example, are scarcely interesting or understandable to a child of 9 or 10, and no good is done by simplifying the whole story so much that the children are given the impression that the war was fought over whether the hair should be worn short or long. From this they could only conclude that their ancestors were lunatics. Most of the great issues of the past, the struggle between Church and State, between King and Barons, between Whig and Tory, between landowners and merchants, between capital and labour, are really outside the understanding of children. Since it is precisely these matters which have been traditionally regarded as the essential subject-matter of history, their disappearance from the syllabus left a vacuum which has not been very satisfactorily filled. In some schools history, as a subject, has disappeared altogether.

If you were to visit a modern primary school you might find any of the following 'situations':

1. History confined to its place in a local or general study, of the kind described above.

2. History taught under such headings as Clothing, Food, Transport. Transport is a particular favourite and for obvious reasons. Coaches, railways, motor-cars, aeroplanes, ships, roads, canals—it is only necessary to mention them to realise what a mine of interest they represent for children and how essential they have been in the story of human progress. There is a wealth of visual material available, photographs, pictures, slides and films, devoted to them. There are museums where their early history can be studied and the modern forms of them are to be seen everywhere. The history of transport is not only technological but human as well, and it is not surprising that many schools make good use of it.

3. Some attention to great personalities. An objection sometimes made to the sort of approach just described is that it leaves out of account the quality of human greatness. This is not altogether true. The figures of Leonardo da Vinci, Drake, James Watt, George Stephenson, the Wright brothers, Brunel, Alcock, Brown and Whittle, to mention only a few who would certainly appear in a history of transport, exhibit this quality. Nevertheless there are other examples of greatness which would not appear in such a history and which many would feel children ought to know, in particular the great humanitarians, Wilberforce, Shaftesbury, Elizabeth Fry, Mary Slessor, Albert Schweitzer. The choice is enormous. The important thing is that children should become aware of the power of the individual human spirit to alter the course of events, to overcome apparently impossible obstacles, to capture the imagination of the many. Later on they will learn the limitations of this power, the importance of team-work, and of economic forces, but if they are without a vision of greatness they will miss an essential experience.

4. Some selected periods of history studied in greater or lesser detail, usually with a strong emphasis on the life of the people. You might, for instance, find such a series as, Life in the Stone Age, Life in Roman Britain, Life in a Norman castle, Life in a 14th-century manor, Life in

Tudor London and so on. Children 'doing' Life in the Stone Age would collect and draw pictures, make models and try their hands at making primitive tools. The task of tying a stone to a stick with string, let alone with strips of hide, to make a hammer gives children a new respect for their ancestors! Most teachers who use this approach find that it works best when done in some detail, and, naturally, that any material drawn from the locality adds greatly to the interest of the work.

5. The use of a time-chart. Children have a very limited sense of past time. They often lump everything before their own days into a very mixed bag called 'the olden days'. There is no general agreement on what should be done about this. Nobody now thinks that learning the dates of the Kings and Queens of England off by heart is a particularly useful exercise, but most would feel that some attempt should be made to help children to arrange what they have studied in order and on a correct scale. The favourite device for doing this is the time-chart which is, in essence, no more than a calibrated straight line, very similar to the number-track described in Chapter 7, on which events and names are filled in at the appropriate point. This will not give to a child a very vivid idea of a century but it can show him that the Peasants' Revolt came before the French Revolution and that the Battle of Waterloo is about the same distance in time from us as it is from the Great Fire of London. A more detailed time-chart for the past, say, 150 years is sometimes used in which personal history can be recorded. For instance:

	1960
I was born	
	1950
	1940
Mother born	
	1930
Father born	
	1920
	1910

Grandfather born	1900
	1890
Great Grandfather born	1880
	1870
	1860
	1850
Great Great Grandfather born	1840
	1830
	1820
Great Great Great Grand-father born	1810

Such a chart can be made personally for and by each child or simply as a general statement of an average state of affairs, and other details such as 'Blériot flew the Channel', 'Wireless telegraphy discovered', 'Manchester–Liverpool railway opened', 'Penny Postage introduced', added as interest or need dictates.

The aim of all this exploration of the world in primary schools is to use the natural curiosity of children to help them to discover how full of interest the world is and to begin to learn how to look at it, what questions to ask about it, how and where to find the answers. This is what being educated is and a child so educated need never be bored or have a dull moment. That is the tremendous objective which the modern primary school has set up.

CHAPTER NINE

A foreign language ?

As recently as 1959 the following words appeared in *Primary Education*, the handbook for teachers published by the Department of Education and Science.[17] 'One suggestion in particular is repeatedly made, that the brighter children at least should begin to learn a foreign language. There are no educational reasons why this should not be, but present conditions of staffing and accommodation often prevent its being done sufficiently well to make the time spent on it worthwhile.' This was a carefully considered statement in a book written by H.M. Inspectors, and in fact, at that date, very few schools included a foreign language in their curriculum, and fewer still kept it there for any length of time.

Five years later, in 1964, a survey showed that French was being taught in 119 L.E.A. areas containing 14,000 primary schools and that of these schools 21% were providing a French course of some kind, 5,000 teachers being involved.[18] This represented a speed of innovation unprecedented in England and Wales, and, since the ways in which changes are brought about are of great interest to parents, a brief description of what happened in those five years may be worth offering.

The great increase in foreign travel which occurred in the 1950s and the growing support for a closer union with other European countries produced a climate of opinion favourable to the learning of a foreign language. The country was ready for it. In 1961–2 the Nuffield Foundation supported some experiments in French teaching in primary schools, one of which, in Leeds, attracted particular attention because of the striking results achieved in a very short time. This led to the

Foundation's approaching the Department with an offer of £100,000 (later increased) to finance a project, designed to discover the feasibility of introducing a foreign language into the curriculum of all primary schools. The experience of the independent preparatory schools had shown that it was perfectly possible to teach a foreign language with success to some children of primary school age. What was not known was whether it was possible to teach one to *all* such children, whether the resources of the teaching body were equal to such an enterprise and what teaching material would be most suitable.

A detailed plan was drawn up in which the Foundation and the Department collaborated. The foundation undertook the research and the work necessary to produce the teaching materials and the Department made the approach to the L.E.A.s and organised the in-service training for the teachers who would like to take part. It was necessary at this early stage to decide which languages were to be used in this project and there was really no possible alternative to French. It was going to be difficult enough to staff the experiment in that language. Any other would have been practically impossible. In any case French is the language of our nearest neighbour, is second only to English as an international tongue, and has a literature unequalled by any of the other possible candidates.

Thirteen areas were chosen for the experiment, namely: Bedfordshire (part), Blackpool, Devon (part), Dorset (part), Durham, Hillingdon (part), Hull, Monmouthshire (part), Northumberland (part), Nottingham, Oxford, Staffordshire (part), West Sussex (part). So many authorities, however, wished to take part that 53 other areas were associated with the experiment and were able to use the teaching material and of course report on results.

By July 1963, the whole scheme was planned, the Nuffield team set to work on the production of the teaching materials, and the Department and the L.E.A.s began the teacher-training programme which included three months in Paris or Besançon for all the teachers concerned. In September 1964 the project was launched, a remarkable feat of organisation which is described more fully in the Schools Council's Field Report No. 2, *French in the Primary School*.

All the 8-year-olds in the pilot areas began French in September 1964. A year later these children started on their second year and a new cohort of 8-year-olds began and in 1966 the process continued. In July 1967 the original cohort will complete the course and, in September, pass into the secondary schools. The Nuffield teaching material was not compulsory. English teachers are never ordered to use a particular book or course. In fact 82% of the teachers in the pilot areas are using the Nuffield material, most of the remainder using a French course called *Bonjour Line* or an American one, *Parlons Français*. It was generally, though not universally agreed that all the work in the first year should be oral, and that reading and writing should not be introduced until the second year. This corresponded to the way in which the children learn their own language, and ensured that they were not introduced to the difficulties of pronouncing French when confronted with the printed word (e.g. 'pain', 'port', 'doigt', 'oignon') until the correct pronunciation had been well established by ear.

While the pilot area schools are following pretty closely the lines laid down in the original plan, there is more variation in the associate areas and, in addition, there are numbers of what are usually called 'free-lance' areas or individual schools which are not associated with the project and follow their own devices. This they are perfectly free to do and there is no essential reason why they should not be doing it well. It must, however, be said that not all of them *are* doing it well and that some are doing it very badly.

Parents, whether their children in primary school are doing French or not, may like to know what are the questions that they would find it useful to ask. You will want to know:

1. Whether the teacher is well enough qualified in the language. To have done O or A level French at school is not good enough by itself. There is no absolute in these matters, but some recent study in France as well as in England is almost indispensable, and to exert pressure on a

school to introduce French if its staff is not qualified is to do your child harm and not good.

2. Whether the course is a suitable one. The three mentioned above, Nuffield, *Bonjour Line* and *Parlons Français*, are all designed for primary children and have all been well tested in use. There are many good courses designed for secondary schools which are no good for younger children. A course devised by the teacher *may* be good, but to frame such a course much more than a good knowledge and command of the language is needed, and few teachers have the necessary linguistic training.

3. Whether the time allowance is suitable. In the early stages of a language a short period (20–30 minutes) every day is best. The difficulties of making a time-table are often formidable and it is not always possible to attain the ideal. If only two long periods, or worse still, one a week can be managed it is better not to do French at all.

4. Whether there is close liaison between the school and *all* the secondary schools to which the children are transferred. Nothing is more disheartening for a child than to study French in the primary school only to find that when he reaches the secondary school his previous study is ignored and he has to start all over again. If the teaching has been inefficient, the course ill-chosen and the time-allowance too meagre, this is unavoidable. The secondary school must begin again and the child may have much to unlearn. If, however, the teaching, the course and the time allowance have been satisfactory, the child will be able to go on where he has left off when he enters the secondary school. Unless arrangements are made for him to do this he will be frustrated and rightly exasperated.

It will be clear from all this that the matter of a foreign language in primary schools is not as simple as it sometimes sounds. It is most unwise for parents to try to persuade a head teacher to introduce French against his better judgment. The right approach is to the L.E.A. It is the L.E.A.'s responsibility to staff the schools. If they are unable to staff your child's school so that a satisfactory course in French can be given, they will explain why and you can then argue the point as you wish. The number of teachers who are really qualified to teach French is limited. As the output of modern language graduates from the universities grows and as the colleges of education expand their modern language teaching, the supply will improve. If this limitation is ignored, if schools try to introduce French before they are properly staffed to do so, the whole of French teaching in Primary Schools may fall into disrepute. The Secondary Schools will be rightly contemptuous and, not for the first time, too much impatience, too much climbing on the band-wagon, will have brought a good idea to disaster.

I have written strongly on this matter because it is those to whom this book is chiefly addressed, the parents and general public, who are entitled to know the facts and whose influence is often decisive. The pilot scheme was carefully devised in order to discover the possibilities and the difficulties, the profit and loss, of introducing French into the primary school. Some encouraging results are already apparent, but it is only when the project is completed and the various objective assessments can be made, that the time will come to decide whether a general expansion is desirable.

CHAPTER TEN

Creating

We saw in Chapter 6 how children learn to write by using their own experience as subject-matter instead of performing exercises. The creative instinct, the desire to make something new for oneself, is universal in man. In primitive times every man and woman satisfied this instinct by making things for their own use. When there were no factories or shops literally everything had to be made by the user. It had to be made well, because a badly-made tool, weapon, or utensil or garment represented a frightful waste of one's own time. Despite the importance of time, many of the objects made were quite intricately decorated. The decorations probably had some magical significance and were thus not just embellishments, but long after their significance had been forgotten, people living in very simple conditions added decoration to whatever they made. A visit to a folk-museum, best of all to an out-door museum such as may be seen in Cardiff, Aarhus, Helsinki and Bucharest, will show how the creative instinct was fulfilled in ordinary daily affairs by peasants and countryfolk generally, to within living memory.

Modern technology and economy has produced a world in which it is possible to buy ready-made almost everything that we need. This is a great convenience and few would really like to go back to a peasant economy, however much they rave about peasant art and crafts. The creative instinct has to find other outlets than building one's own house, making one's own tools, weaving one's own cloth. The enormous increase of amateur gardening and 'do-it-yourself' is partly, of course, an economic phenomenon, but no one can doubt that they satisfy the creative instinct of those who do them. The development of musical activities, classical and popular, and the demand for evening classes in art, sculpture, pottery, weaving and embroidery are more evidence of how strong is the need to make new things for oneself. A great deal of technical work of course satisfies this need, but mass-production and automation decreases the satisfaction, and a man who has spent his day in a joinery manufacturer's may well go at once to his own little workshop when he has had his tea.

In spite of this clear evidence that creation is a human need, there are still some who question the importance and even the presence of art and music, dance and drama in the primary school curriculum. Everything that we know about human beings generally, and children in particular, points to the importance of the arts in education. They are the language of a whole range of human experience and to neglect them is to neglect ourselves.

This little introduction will certainly not convince any reader who seriously doubts the truth of its contention, but it may indicate to others the ground on which the arts have a place in the school curriculum. They are not 'frills' but essentials just as much as the 3 Rs. In one sense indeed they are more essential for, while for almost the whole of his existence man has done without the 3 Rs, he has never, so far as we know, done without art.

In this chapter I shall describe what is going on today in the fields of art, craft and music, leaving drama and dance to a later chapter. This happens to be a convenient way of dividing them up, but all are equally important as creative activities and so is the writing of prose and poetry which I have already discussed.

It was in the teaching of art that the revolution which this book describes really began, and it owed its origin very largely to one person whom I have already mentioned in Chapter 1. Marion Richardson was an art teacher at Dudley High School in Worcestershire and, later, an Inspector of Art under the old London County Council. When she began her work in London in 1930 art in elementary schools was unspeakably dull. It consisted mainly of drawing models with an HB pencil. Such colour as was used was water-colour (a notoriously difficult and subtle medium to handle) and this was applied to drawings of plants. Drawing paper was used and, since this was very expensive and requisition funds were limited, it was cut up into small rectangles 8 in. × 5 in. or even less. Very few children were capable of using these materials and limitations creatively.

Marion Richardson encouraged the use of large sheets of cheap paper (sometimes even old newspapers were used), of large brushes which would hold plenty of colour, of powder paints which were cheap to use and could produce solid masses of colour, and she suggested that the children should be allowed to paint what they liked and not be given subjects or models. The results of this, as it then seemed, wildly revolutionary policy was that young children began to produce paintings which many adult critics found very exciting. They typically set about painting a picture without a moment's pause, with extraordinary confidence and apparently with a clear purpose in their minds. Anyone who has watched infants painting must have noticed this. They clearly enjoyed laying on colour in thick daubs and, since they represented everything symbolically, they had no concern with correct drawing or perspective.

This method of teaching or of allowing art spread pretty rapidly and it was developed in the 1930s and after the war, by an increasing number of teachers. Fundamentally Marion Richardson's principles remain unchallenged but once the breakthrough was made all sorts of refinements began to appear. The very free, bold use of bright paints that had characterised the early work and is still found in the infants' schools, began to give way to closer observation, and more subtle colouring. As early as 1933 there was a young teacher called Robin Tanner in an elementary school in Wiltshire whose children did four large murals on their classroom wall, representing the four seasons. They had never seen any reproductions of modern painting but it was of Stanley and Gilbert Spencer and of Paul Nash that the visitor was reminded. Subsequently Tanner became an H.M.I. and perhaps had more influence on the development than anyone else. He encouraged the use of a much more subtle palette and in particular of the 'dirty' colours, browns and ochres and greys, the colours of bark and lichen and dead grass, and thus of a much more perceptive vision in children. This was also shown in a return to the drawing of plants and shells and stones with exact observation and a most careful delineation and colouring. This did not rule out the free and inventive kind of painting which itself developed, as new techniques and tools and more ambitious subject-matter were tried, but it did make the work more varied and thus more adaptable to individual tastes and capacities.

Only a large number of very expensive coloured illustrations to this book could give the reader any idea of the kind of work that primary children now do, but exhibitions of children's paintings are frequently held in individual schools, in L.E.A. offices and nationally, and these offer an easy means of seeing it.

Since a large proportion of adults are apt to say, 'I can't draw or paint', it may be worth emphasising that every child can. There are a few children who can never learn to read and rather more for whom reading will always be something of a struggle, but some of the most interesting art is to be found in schools for the mentally handicapped, who often exhibit as much confidence and purposefulness when they are painting as is shown by clever children. So far from art being a special language for the few, it is a universal language which all children can use.

Handicraft for primary children, thirty years ago, usually consisted of making raffia mats, and cardboard models, with needlework for girls. Change here has come more slowly than in painting and there are still many schools in which the craft work offers very limited scope either for inventiveness or for learning useful skills. Where change is taking place it seems to be in the following directions:

1. Infants' schools lay particular stress on inventiveness. They collect pieces of wood of all sizes and in fact almost any junk that you can think of and supply the children with hammers, nails and small saws. With this cheap and simple equipment the children construct the most surprising and

sometimes elaborate objects. Just as their paintings are symbolic, not representational, these structures that they make are not models but flights of the imagination. Many show extraordinary ingenuity and some are so large and complex that they may take a whole term to complete. The children will tell you that they are castles, or spaceships, or trains. They know very well what they are doing, though it may not be immediately apparent to the adult eye.

This kind of craft is found mainly in infants' schools but it is really just as appropriate to older children who, if given the same opportunities will gradually acquire more skill, find out how to solve more difficult problems, e.g. making and mounting wheels, and discover what can be done and what cannot. They will thus come quite naturally to the stage when, in the secondary school if not before, they are ready to learn a traditional craft such as joinery or turning with all its disciplines. I can think of one boy who is now a very skilled craftsman in wood, metal and clay who, as a little boy, was always making fantastic objects in which inventiveness ran far ahead of technical knowledge or achievement. What a mistake it would have been to teach him too early and thus deprive him of this imaginative period and make him grow up before he was ready.

Some teachers were hesitant, when this kind of craft was first talked of, about giving tools to children with which they might hurt themselves or each other. No one in their senses would give chisels or bradawls to children, or heavy hammers and saws which they could not handle, but a light hammer and a small coarse-toothed saw can both be handled quite efficiently even by 4-year-olds and experience has shown that accidents are very rare and never serious.

2. The traditional crafts which seem to fit most happily into the primary school of today are those connected with fabrics. A good many country schools investigate the whole process of producing woollen cloth. They begin by collecting from the hedges and wire fences all the sheeps'

wool that they can find. They wash it, card it and spin it using home-made implements at each stage. They collect the necessary flowers and berries and roots for making different coloured dyes. The wool is dyed and mordanted (their first introduction to chemistry). It is woven on home-made looms and sometimes on much bigger looms which have been discarded from industry and re-erected in the school. Schools in towns or in other areas where there are no sheep cannot do all this but they can and do experiment with block-printing and tie-dyeing ready-made fabrics of cotton and linen. The block may be of wood or cut in potato and all sorts of experiments with different surfaces and substances may be tried. The results may often be seen in the form of curtains for the classroom, covers for books and sometimes of summer dresses worn by the girls.

Children taught in this way rediscover the lost delight of making things for themselves. Few of them, when they grow up, will perhaps continue to make things. They will buy them ready-made from shops like everyone else, but they will have had an experience which will have opened their eyes to the possibilities of texture, colour, and pattern, and they will become more discriminating buyers, less ready to accept the badly-designed and the ugly, more conscious of beauty in everyday things.

3. Another craft that has recently developed considerably in primary schools is modelling in clay or chalk or wood. Try taking a big lump of potter's clay yourself, put it on a board in front of you and press your fingers into it. You will at once want to make a shape. You will pull it and push it and you will make something—a head, a face, a house, a tree, an animal—however crude and 'bad' you may think it. No one, least of all children, can resist doing this with clay if they are given the chance. From the day they arrived in the nursery school, or in the reception class in the infants' school, many children will have had clay to mess about with and clay modelling is simply an extension of what began in this way. Children often show remarkable skill as well as feeling in their handling of clay and

no one who has seen them at work can doubt that, like painting, this is a 'language' which they can use and understand.

The making of shapes by cutting away, that is carving or sculpture, is more difficult for children than building them up in clay, and stone is not often found in primary schools. Lumps of chalk, however, are soft enough to be cut with a knife without the use of hammer and chisel, and in some schools this craft has been tried with success. Wood is rather more of a problem, particularly because the close-grained woods which are most suitable for carving are the hardest. Some schools have used the soft woods with good results, and there is something about whittling away at a piece of wood with a knife which is very satisfying, especially perhaps to boys. An interesting example of this is to be found in a small school on the north Cornish coast. The beach is a few yards from the school gate and on it is usually a considerable quantity of drift wood, already made barkless and hard by the action of the sea. The shapes of this wood are interesting in themselves and the boys of the school (the girls are not interested) collect the wood and work on it, not with knives, but with Surform files, and adapt it, sometimes into a semblance of human or animal figures, and sometimes into abstract forms of extraordinary beauty.

4. Clay is also used in primary schools for the ancient craft of pottery. The craft of 'throwing' pots, that is of turning them on a wheel, is really too difficult for young children and, since wheels are expensive, it is rarely practised in primary schools. The modern electric kiln in which the pots are baked is also expensive though occasionally to be found. The built-up pot, whether slab or coil, however, is well within the powers of children and a remarkably efficient kiln can be made with nothing more elaborate than bricks and sawdust. The making and decorating of built-up pots and firing them in a home-made kiln requires a combination of inventiveness, skill and technical knowledge in proportions which makes it a good craft for children.

5. Needlework was established in the elementary schools very early in their history. It was considered essential that every girl should be able to ply her needle so that she could make clothes for herself and her family when she grew up. Long after modern technology and marketing had made it possible to buy cheap and well-made shirts, petticoats, knickers and frocks, these four garments continued to form the main content of elementary school needlework. Only gradually have they been banished or put in their proper place. The two most noticeable changes are, first, that the dismal white cotton and calico have gone, and that the emphasis is now on decorative needlework and simple embroidery, with the use of coloured wools and cottons and silks and on invididual designs instead of transferred commercial patterns; secondly, that needlework is no longer so rigidly confined to girls. This may sound strange to many masculine ears, but, if it is considered in relation to what was said in Section 1 above, it may be more comprehensible. The junk that is collected by the infants' schools will include fabrics of various kinds and sizes, and these are often incorporated into the structures that the children invent. A darning-needle and thread will then be added to the hammer, the nails and the saw and are just as likely to be used by the boys as by the girls, just as the girls will certainly not leave the hammers and saws to the boys. Later on, under social pressure, most of the boys may come to regard needlework as 'not for them' but this represents a completely out-of-date view of the roles of men and women and perhaps it will become, in time, obsolete.

Music, like craft, has been practised for a very long time in schools for young children. Originally, when there were only church schools, this may have been done with an eye on the choir, but from the earliest days national, patriotic songs were taught and, until recently, though the repertory had been greatly increased, music was mainly a matter of singing. The singing of a song can be just as creative as composing one and singing will always, it is to be hoped, be given an important place in the education of English children. The folk-songs of England, rescued in the nick of time by Cecil Sharp from total oblivion, provide a splendid repertory in themselves. Tunes such as *The Lark in the Morn, I will give my love an apple, Searching for Lambs* and *Waley, Waley up the bank*, are some of the most lovely in the world, and others such as *The Drummer and the Cook, Seventeen come Sunday*, and *'A-rovin'* are rousing songs which never fail to delight singer and hearer. These and many others belong to our heritage and the children must never be deprived of them, however much they are added to by new composers and songs from other countries. Many of them come from particular parts of the country. Somerset has produced an exceptionally large number of good songs, and it would be surprising if schools in that county undertaking local studies did not include in them, in some way, the folk-songs and dances of the region. I can remember one, in an area particularly rich in good tunes, which had a repertory consisting solely of John Peel, but I expect that things are now very different.

The most interesting innovation that has taken place in recent years has been the introduction into the primary schools of instrumental music. In the 1930s it was quite common to find percussion bands in the infants' schools and at their best these were a good introduction to reading music in staff notation and to listening to, and taking some part in, music of good quality. If you had to count 12 bars of a Handel Minuet before striking your triangle on the first beat of the 13th bar, you listened to Handel as never before! Too often, however, neither the instruments nor the music were of good enough quality and, despite some splendid work here and there, the percussion band had not the success that was hoped for it. A less common instrumental introduction at that period was the bamboo pipe. This was, in theory at any rate, constructed by the children themselves and provided, thus, a training in handicraft and much useful ear-training since the pipes had to be tuned to the diatonic scale. This never caught on very widely despite the enthusiasm of the devotees and the help and advice given by the Pipers' Guild, a private organisation with a sadly small membership. The pipe has now given way to the Recorder, a rather more sophisticated instrument, formerly used in the orchestra, which is commercially manufactured and which, having much the same fingering as the Flute, is a good introduction to that instrument. This instrument which includes four members, the Descant, the Treble, the Tenor and the Bass, has given to a substantial number of children the opportunity of serious instrumental music-making in the primary school, but it is not easy to learn and usually only a small proportion of children in any one school learn it. Something more was needed.

The percussion instruments of the old percussion band— the drum, the tambourine, the triangle, the castanets and the jingle-bells—could not vary their pitch. Each one played the same note all the time and it was only the rhythm that could be varied. There are, however, some percussion instruments which do have a variable pitch and can thus play tunes—Glockenspiels, Xylophones, Chime-bars and some others which had been forgotten save as words in the Old Testament. The great German teacher of music Carl Orff used these and it was his influence which brought them into use on the continent and indirectly into the British Isles. These instruments are comparatively easy to play and they allow children to do, in music, what they were already doing in writing and art and craft—namely experiment, trying out their own ideas, make something new, in a word compose. They have another advantage. They are tuned to the diatonic scale, that is the kind of scale that you get if you play all the white notes on the piano starting at C, but the bars, etc., are not fixed in position and by taking out two of them, the third and the seventh, you produce the pentatonic scale, which is the kind of scale that you get if you play all the black notes. A great many Scottish folk-songs, like *The Boatman* and *Colin's Cattle*, are in this scale. Apart from its inherent beauty it has the great advantage that no discords are possible in it, and two children playing on different instruments tuned to it, can produce pleasant harmonic effects and thus begin to create harmonically and not only melodically.

None of this alters the fact that in order to learn the pianoforte or the violin or the flute, or any of the classical instruments, a pupil must undergo a long and arduous training. It is interesting that the development has been accompanied by an increasing demand among primary school children for lessons in these much more difficult instruments. Most of this demand is met by private teaching, but it is becoming much less rare than it was to find a string class, and sometimes a pianoforte class, being taken in a primary school, usually by a visiting teacher. Far from encouraging a sloppy, uncritical attitude to music, the experimental method seems to be stimulating children to tackle the stern discipline of instrumental playing.

Although this chapter is entitled 'creating' and Chapter 9 'A foreign language' and Chapter 8 'Exploring the World', it must be clear that creating new things is a way of exploring the world, of finding out the possibilities of materials as well as of oneself and that learning a foreign language is another way. In fact, at every point in this book it is clear that every 'subject' both serves and is served by others. We cannot include everything in the school curriculum. We saw, particularly in Chapter 8, how much indeed we have to leave out. What must be preserved, however, is the balance so that all the essential ingredients are there. One of these is creativeness.

CHAPTER ELEVEN

Body and soul

Many years ago some enlightened education authorities introduced school dinners. The aim was to counter the malnutrition and even sheer hunger from which too many of the poorer children suffered. Perhaps inevitably but none the less unfortunately, an atmosphere of the poor law institution hung about much of this provision. The food was cooked, sometimes the day before, in central kitchens and distributed in containers to inelegantly named 'feeding centres', where it was served with little regard for good manners or style. I can recall visiting such a centre in 1938 in a northern city. It was in a disused laundry, unadapted save for bare trestle tables and backless forms. The children sat in silence under the supervision of a very minor official who bellowed with rage at any sign of conversation and was understandably terrified of the 100 or so children who, unwashed and uninstructed, sat gobbling the stew which had been put before them.

Not all feeding centres were as bad as that one, but it was very difficult to establish decent standards of cooking, serving or eating in the conditions that were then general. During the war the Ministry took over central responsibility for school meals and a tremendous drive ensued to set up good kitchens, wherever possible on school premises, and good dining conditions where a meal as a social occasion became a possibility. School meals are now almost universal. The parents pay the cost price of the food, or, in cases of need, less than this or nothing at all. The Department have complete financial responsibility but the L.E.A.s administer the arrangements locally.

Both in standard of provision and in quality of cooking there is a good deal of variety as between areas and between

one school and another. I have eaten many school dinners in
my time and have fared well and badly. At its best a school
meal can be a civilised and enjoyable gathering, teachers and
children sitting down together to eat well-cooked and well-
served food. This is the ideal and it is one that some schools
attained many years ago. In the town mentioned above
there was, at the same epoch, an elementary school headmaster of the old type (Boys' Department) who organised
his own school dinner, over which he presided at a high
table surrounded by his senior boys and which was conducted with a decorum and a style which the grammar
school, two streets away, could not match!

In Chapter One I described the change that took place in
the 1930s from the old Drill to a more active and varied type
of Physical Education. Since the war a significant, though still
small, proportion of primary schools have gone a great deal
further and have broken away from the set exercises almost
completely. Once again it was the infants' schools which
showed the way. Shortly before the war climbing frames
began to appear in a few of the most enlightened schools and
it was noticeable that the children needed no instruction as
to what to do on them. They discovered their possibilities
for themselves and used them to discover their own capabili-
ties and limitations. Furthermore, they almost never had an
accident. They seemed to know instinctively when they had
reached a height or a position which represented for them a
limit. The climbing nets, used for commando training during
the war, when they became available as surplus stock,
provided another stage in this free, exploratory kind of
physical activity. If your children are lucky enough to be able
to climb trees you will have noticed all this yourself, the way
in which they discover what they can do and learn by
experience how to do it. But town children cannot climb
trees and get into trouble if they try, and if they climb on
buildings or railway cuttings run into serious danger. The
new apparatus made available to all children what had only
been possible hitherto for the fortunate few.

The increase in camping, mountain-walking, and sailing
that has taken place since the war has also had its influence in

primary schools, though its main strength has naturally been among older children. Many schools organise their own expeditions to wild country and, provided that these are carefully and sensibly planned, they provide ideal experience for the children, in which physical exercise, initiative and enjoyment of the country and/or the water are combined. One of my own children climbed Wetherlam (2,510 ft.) when he was 5, and another Scafell Pike (3,210 ft.) when she was 6. The capacities of young children are greater than is often supposed but it is extremely important that expeditions of this kind should be undertaken only under the control of experienced mountaineers with proper clothing and equipment. The same applies to all activities in which any element of risk is even remotely involved. With proper precautions there is no reason why primary school children should not begin to learn the skills and experience the pleasures of camping, climbing and boating.

A third influence which has made for change in physical education in primary schools is what is usually described as Movement, with a capital M. The originator of this was Rudolf Laban. In the course of some time-and-motion studies that he was doing in a German factory, Laban became interested in the movements of the human body and undertook an exhaustive study of them. The Nazi persecution brought him and some of his co-workers to England just before the war and his principles and methods began to be adopted in a few primary schools. Even before 1945 there were some schools in Manchester and elsewhere which practised them, and latterly they have spread widely, with particular concentrations in the West Riding and Oxfordshire.

It is not easy to describe a Movement session to someone who has not seen one. Readers who were fortunate enough to see the B.B.C. series *Experience and Discovery* which was telecast in 1965-6, will remember the activity work done by the Bristol Infant School and the West Riding Junior School shown on the reel devoted to Movement. Even that was only one aspect of Movement. Briefly, it begins by being an exploration of the body's capacities for movement, heavy and light, large and small, fast and slow, with the whole body involved. The teacher suggests and comments but the interpretation of his suggestions is left to the children. He may say, for instance: 'Start making big, strong, slow movements, using your legs and arms and hands and heads. Try to use all the space around you, above your head, close to the floor. Now find a partner and make your movement into a response to his, so that you are aware of what he is doing as well as yourself. Now speed the movements up. Make them sharper, more jerky'. The children respond to these suggestions but none does the same thing. As time goes on control of the body develops and the children are able to perform a very wide range of movements, with confidence and grace, both singly, in pairs and in groups, the pairs and groups forming and disintegrating as the movement demands.

The point of all this may perhaps be most easily grasped if we consider ourselves, particularly those of us who are past our first youth. How many of us feel awkward, clumsy, self-conscious and embarrassed if we are called upon to perform any movement to which we are not accustomed? How many of us have watched with envy the apparently effortless ease with which expert riders, skiers, fencers, divers, dancers, potters, woodcutters, etc. move their bodies and compared it with our own ineptitude? If we watch other people doing nothing more unusual than walking, how many do it really well and how many with an ungainly carriage or stride? The fact is that most of us are pretty inefficient movers and that many of us cannot perform even the most ordinary movements really well.

The object of Movement in school is to provide a basic training in control of the body so that all movements may be improved and so that the specialised movements required for particular sports and crafts may be more easily learned. There is no question of its taking the place of organised games which will always appeal to at least the older juniors, but it must be said that too much emphasis on competitive team games at the junior stage is undesirable. The great games tradition of England has sometimes led to this happening, and for every Test Match player who was taught the strokes

by his father at the age of 7 there must be 1,000 non-cricketers
who gave up the game because it was forced upon them too
early. Even worse has been the effect of junior school league
football which has too often resulted in too much com-
petitiveness and too little sportsmanship and even in premature "scouting" by professional clubs. These evils can be
avoided but too often they are not.

I shall return to movement later, but a word must first be
said about a sport which has made great strides in primary
schools since the war, namely swimming. This is a splendid
sport for children. There are certainly risks but if proper
training is given and proper safety precautions taken these
are very small, and, as the number of public baths grows, the
opportunities for pursuing it after schooldays are over are
much greater than they used to be.

In a number of schools in London and elsewhere you will
find small learning baths. Some of these fit into large disused
classrooms. They are completely safe and can be used even
by infants. When the element of fear is removed by the use of
very shallow water little children learn very quickly indeed
and 100% success is quite common. The water can be heated
and chlorinated quite easily when the bath is small, and the
children can even test the chlorine content themselves
before each bathe by the very simple device of comparing
the colour of a specimen of the water with that of a bottle in
which the proportions are correct.

At a great many county and suburban schools there is room
for an outdoor bath and this is something which the parents
often present to the school. On summer evenings a gang of
fathers may be found at work digging or bulldozing or
mixing concrete or installing chlorination plants, a form of
parental co-operation which is immensely appreciated by
staff and children. Since there is little or no cost of labour
and quite frequently some or all of the machinery required
can be provided by a parent, the cost of such pools can be
very modest. If they were supplied by the Education
Authorities they would have to be constructed by a con-
tractor and the cost borne by the ratepayers and taxpayers.
When the parents are able to undertake the construction

themselves they save their own money (though not of course
their time!) and provide their children with a wonderful
advantage that they might otherwise not have.

What we have been considering so far in this chapter is
the various activities undertaken by children which develop
the strength, endurance, control and skilful use of the body.
All these activities require the individual co-operation of each
child. None can be reduced to the rigid mechanical drill
(arms stretch! knees bend!) which was common forty years
ago. But there is more to it than this.

Movement is as much the basis of dance and ballet and
drama as it is of football, swimming and ski-ing, and Movement in the Laban sense has developed in an artistic direction as well as in a more purely acrobatic one. It is interesting
that in the United States this artistic movement has led to the
creation of a professional art-form with which the dis-
tinguished name of Martha Graham is associated, but there
has been little or no use of it in education. In Great Britain
the opposite has happened. No professional art-form has so
far emerged, but there has been an exciting development in
primary education. Once again, this is difficult to describe.
The basic training in movement described above is the
foundation for a kind of ballet or dance-drama devised by
the children themselves. They may take a well-known story
such as *The Pied Piper* or such an incident as *The Jabberwock*
from *Alice through the Looking Glass* or they may invent a
story or situation of their own, and interpret it by movement,
usually without speech but sometimes with the use of percussion instruments, especially drums and tambourines.

Those teachers who are the most dedicated followers of
Laban believe that all dramatic work with young children
should derive from the movement of the body and that
appeals to the imagination, such as would be made at a
school of dramatic art, are mistaken. It is unnecessary to go
into the arguments here. A great many teachers do make use
of the imagination, including many who admire and make use
of many of Laban's ideas. What is now generally agreed is
that the traditional dramatic performance involving the
learning of parts and a stage with lighting and a proscenium

arch, culminating in a public performance, is unsuitable for young children. It requires powers of interpreting somebody else's words and of character-drawing that few children possess, and a technical skill and deftness which are equally rare. It is in a convention—the picture stage—which is very difficult for children to understand and it almost inevitably leads to intensive coaching of the few able children and to boredom if not neglect for the remainder. It is true that there are a few exceptional teachers who can bring it off, but at a heavy cost to all concerned, and I hope that if you find that there is no 'school play' at your children's primary school you will not be disappointed.

The kind of drama which is gaining favour, whether it is pure Laban or not, is that in which the whole floor space of hall or gymnasium is used, with very simple lighting and props and sometimes no special costumes. If there is a performance at all it is a very informal occasion, on which the parents come to see what their children are doing. The 'play' may again be a legend or story on which the children and their teacher have been working. The incidents as well as the treatment will have been discussed with the children and many of their ideas will have been incorporated. The teacher will have been a co-ordinator but certainly not a 'producer' in the sense in which that word is understood in the theatre. What the parents see is a piece of work in progress, not a finished production.

The most popular dramatic work for primary children is still probably the Christmas Nativity play and it is too often a failure, for the reasons just given against the set play. If the children are allowed to think a Nativity play out for themselves, in consultation with their teacher, they may produce something very beautiful and moving, but there are foolish people who might think what they did was irreverent or unorthodox, and most teachers play for safety and either choose a set play or do not do one at all.

In an earlier chapter we saw how important play is in the development of young children. Drama is a form of play. In it you pretend to be someone else and if you are going to do that well you must feel what it is like to be that person and in fact become him while the play lasts. All who have acted in amateur productions will know that, quite early on in the rehearsal stage, the actors begin to address each other off the stage by their play-names and keep this up until after the performance. This they do quite unprompted and it is a device to help them to *be* their parts. Drama is a way of extending experience by becoming another person and by finding out what it is like to be in a particular situation which may be very different from one's real-life one. In a great play the actors are caught up into the pattern of the drama as into a religious ritual.

Drama is religious in origin, and religious ritual is dramatic. All primitive drama is religious in subject-matter and even the modern secular drama has something religious about it. Religion is an attempt to find a pattern in the universe, in history, in human affairs. Drama is an attempt to arrange human affairs so that they make a cohesive pattern. So is poetry—so is all art. But drama has the special characteristic of allowing, demanding even, a personal participation, or impersonation.

It is possible that if religious education in primary schools was approached through drama many of the difficulties surrounding it would disappear. The children would take the great stories of the Creation, of the separation of God and Man, of Incarnation and Redemption, of the Good Samaritan and the Prodigal Son and would act them as stories in their own way, learning through this the meaning of wonder and worship, of evil and repentance, of compassion and callousness. There would be some for whom this complex of lived and acted experience only made sense if they came to believe in a power of goodness which transcended time and space and yet was immanent in it. These would, as they grew older, ask for instruction in the Christian faith and it would be a faith into which they had grown. I believe that there would be a great many of these, but others, who could not accept the idea of God, would have had the experience, would understand something of what religion was really about and be rescued from the more arid and negative kind of unbelief and from the 'couldn't care less' attitude that

goes with it. Neither the ultimate believer nor the ultimate
unbeliever would have to face the destructive experience of
rejecting, or finding it difficult not to reject as fairy-tales,
stories which had been taught to them as history.

That is a personal pipe-dream. What actually happens in
the religious education period in primary schools is very
different. R.E. is the only subject which is compulsory.[19]
This is a matter of history. Until 1870 all schools were
denominational and naturally taught religion. When the non-
denominational schools were established the great majority
of the parents who used them wanted religion taught. There
was a lot of squabbling about exactly what was to be taught
and this eventually led to what are known as Agreed
Syllabuses, that is syllabuses of religious instruction agreed
between teachers and representatives of the Church of
England and of the Free Churches. The point was simply
that the syllabus should not contain any doctrine or dogma
which could affront the conscience of any Christian. The
Roman Catholics took no part in the drawing up of any of
these agreed syllabuses because they objected to any religious
instruction which departed positively or negatively from the
doctrines of Rome. A conscience clause in the Act of 1870,
repeated ever since, allowed teachers who objected on conscientious grounds to opt out of religious teaching and parents
who objected for the same reason to withdraw their children.
Very little use has ever been made of this clause. Teachers
who were unbelievers either taught with their tongues in their
cheeks or emphasised the non-theological parts of the
syllabus. Parents who were unbelievers nearly always took
the easy way out and spared the school and the child the
embarrassment of withdrawal. This not very satisfactory
or creditable state of affairs was probably fairly widespread
and was by no means confined to the undenominational
schools. There were of course many teachers in both kinds
of school who were devout and practising Christians and
some of them took religious education very seriously. Too
many, however, had little idea of how to teach it and often
fell back on old-fashioned methods which they would have
despised in other subjects.

Recently several developments have upset the delusive calm of the situation just described. First, unbelief has become respectable and unbelievers rather more aggressive about their rights. The humanist voice is certainly louder than it was, though it is difficult to know how strong the opposition really is. Whenever opinion polls are taken among parents, it invariably emerges that a huge majority of them (80% or more) want their children to receive religious instruction in school.[20] Some reasonable doubt may be felt about the strength of conviction behind some of this majority, but no contrary evidence has so far come to light. The humanist case has been very well and moderately put in the Plowden Report and readers who are interested are referred to it there.[21] The most damaging attack, however, has come from the Christian side.[22] The researches of Professor Goldman of Didsbury have shown that a great many religious concepts which have been gaily taught to young children for generations are incomprehensible to them and that religious instruction in primary schools may be doing more harm than good to the cause of religion. This is partly because of bad teaching but it is also because of the nature of the material taught. If children are taught concepts before they can understand them they will form distorted pictures of what is being taught and will reject the teaching when they come to realise how absurd it was, not absurd in itself, but absurd in the form in which it reached the child.

The present position then is that the whole question of what ought to be taught to children must be re-examined, and that much that is in the agreed syllabus and, of course, in the denominational syllabuses ought to be revised or removed altogether. This will not be easy to achieve. In the meantime, however, it remains true that the best religious instruction comes, as it always has, from believing and practising parents. These are not without their problems and they often need instruction themselves! But they and the ministers of their church are likely to make a better job of it than most schools.

Not only is religious education compulsory by law but all schools are required to hold what is called 'an Act of

Worship' and to hold it at the beginning of every day.[23] The
Conscience clause operates here too with the same almost
non-existent effect. The name usually given to this Act of
Worship is Assembly. Many schools take a great deal of
trouble with it. It nearly always includes three elements—
hymns, prayers and a reading, often from the Bible but
sometimes from other sources. It is sometimes conducted by
the head teacher, sometimes by a member of the staff
and sometimes by the children themselves. All Christians
would agree that instruction without worship is not religion
at all, though few would think that a daily assembly at
school, however well planned and conducted, is a sub-
stitute for private prayer and worship in church or chapel.
For many children the daily Assembly is the only worship
that they know and Christians must be grateful to the
teachers who take such pains to make it genuinely devout.
Sometimes it is trivial and sentimental, but only rarely
perfunctory. At some schools it is attended by a few parents,
at others local ministers are invited from time to time to
conduct it. In the church school it is often taken by the parish
priest, or his curate. In schools where none of the staff are
practising Christians it is often, inevitably, a secular gathering the merits of which all would recognise, though to a
Christian it falls short of what an assembly should be.

It is perhaps not entirely surprising that the state of change
in religious education should be more chaotic and uncertain
than in any other part of the curriculum. This simply
reflects the adult world, which is less sure of itself in the
realm of values, and of the nature of man and the universe,
than it is of any other branch of knowledge. There is a lot of
work to be done by everybody.

CHAPTER TWELVE

Who is to guard the guardians ? *

It has been made clear at many points in this book that the English primary teacher carries a heavy weight of responsibility. In other countries teachers are, to a greater or lesser extent, told what to teach and how to teach it, what text-book to use and how much time to spend on each subject. In England, as we have seen, all this is in practice under the control of each individual head teacher and a good deal of it is decided by the individual class-teacher. Many American exchange teachers are bewildered when they are not handed a 'programme' for their classes, and even English people are frequently astonished when they realise how little general direction there is in English schools.

Parents may well feel some misgivings about this. Those who are obliged to move house while their children are at school are quite reasonably afraid that a change of subject-matter as well as of method may mean a setback at an important stage. Quite apart from this, it may be thought that, although the best teachers will use their liberty well and justify the responsibility laid on them, there will be some, perhaps quite a number, who would do better with more precise guidance. Many foreign educationalists are quite frank in saying that they regard our system as anarchic and are convinced that its undoubted success with some must be balanced by failure with others.

We have seen in Chapter 1 that the present system evolved gradually from a very different state of affairs in which teachers *were* directed and obliged to follow a

---

* This is a translation of a sentence by the poet Juvenal. He was writing about the difficulty of guarding an attractive wife, but the quotation is now often used in the sense intended in this chapter.

'programme'. The change that has taken place has been tested at each stage as more and more liberty (and responsibility) has been granted to the teacher. Behind it has been, first, the conviction that a teacher will do his best work if he is given the opportunity to use his initiative and judgment at every point and that when much is demanded much will be given. Secondly, all that we know of children's development and nature points to the need for an individual approach. No programme, however brilliantly or expertly devised, can suit every child and only somebody in close touch with him can decide what is best for him.

No system of education is perfect and it is a matter for discussion whether the advantages claimed for the English one outweigh its disadvantages. It is undoubtedly true that there are some teachers who might do better if they were spoon-fed and it is undoubtedly true that English children who change school constantly probably suffer more than children in countries where they can be sure of picking up everything in the new school just where they left it in the old. Readers of this book will have to decide, on the evidence before them, whether I am right in upholding the English system and they will want to know whether there are any checks at all upon what goes on in the schools. The law (i.e. the Education Act of 1944) is so general and even vague in its educational terms that it hardly constitutes a check on curriculum or method.[24] There are, however, three organisations which do constitute checks, though that is not their sole function, and which are essential parts of the English system.

The oldest of them, is Her Majesty's Inspectorate of Schools, founded in 1839. This is a national body numbering 495 for England and 48 for Wales, appointed by the Queen in Council but operating under the authority of the Secretary of State for Education. The head of the body, the Senior Chief Inspector, is directly responsible to the Permanent Under Secretary of State and is comparable in rank to the Deputy Under Secretary. The inspectorate is spread throughout the country. They are not 'gentlemen from Whitehall'. Most of them live in the area in which they work and spend about ten years in a district before being moved to another. They include men and women and every variety of educational experience and qualification, and all of them have been teachers themselves. About 300 of them are mainly or partially concerned with primary schools and each has a varying number of schools assigned to him.

The first duty of an inspector, or H.M.I. as he is always called, is to know his schools. How often he visits them, how long he spends in each and what he does when he gets there are left to him to decide. From time to time he may write a report on the school which is sent to the D.E.S. who issue it to the school and to the L.E.A., but he will always write some notes on the school for his own use and for that of other colleagues who may visit it. Since inspectors are organised in teams the inspector to whom a school is assigned will always be able to obtain the help of colleagues who may be more expert in some particular subject or aspect of the school than he is.

What do teachers, and through them, the children gain from H.M.I.'s visits? First and most obviously the teachers gain from having their work seen by, and being able to discuss it with, someone who is a teacher himself, who has seen the work of many other teachers and schools and who is not an employee of the L.E.A. The Inspectorate is much sought after and is able to recruit its members from a vast number of applicants. It is very proud of its traditions of independent professional judgment and of its high standards. It can offer to teachers a service which helps them to keep up to date, to see their work through the eyes of someone with a wider knowledge than their own, and to know what experiments have been tried elsewhere and how they have fared.

H.M.I. inspects the whole school. He is concerned with the building and everything in it; nothing is considered outside his scope. He never says: 'This is not my job'. If he finds anything in the building or its surroundings, in the teaching, the furniture, the equipment, the books, which he thinks is harmful to the children he draws attention to it. H.M.I. has no direct powers. He cannot tell the head teacher what to do, or order an improvement to the premises, but he can and does report his findings to the Department, the L.E.A., the school managers, and last but not least to the school staff. He is completely independent of the L.E.A. and at the same time, because he lives where he works, he can often help the Department to appreciate the local attitude to particular questions.

He will spend most of his time either talking to the head teacher or in the classrooms, looking at the children's work, talking to them and to their teachers, listening to what is going on, with the intention of helping and advising but never of directing or forbidding. Moreover he tries to suit what he says to the particular circumstances of the school. He does not go round preaching a doctrine. He knows it is no use trying to revolutionise the practice of an elderly teacher nearing retirement who would only be disheartened by advice which, by implication, told her that everything she was doing was out of date. He knows that a young teacher in his first year is more likely to need encouragement than admonition. He works by influence not by authority.

H.M.I.'s influence is not mediated solely through his visits to schools. The most important other way in which it operates is through short courses. These are refresher courses for teachers organised by the D.E.S. and staffed almost entirely by H.M.I.s. There are over 100 of these courses arranged annually for teachers in all kinds of schools and they last usually for about ten days each. They cover all subjects and all phases of education and they are so popular that it is becoming increasingly impossible to satisfy even a fraction of the demand for them. Since they depend for their quality upon H.M.I.'s knowledge of schools, they cannot be increased in number, without making too heavy demands on H.M.I.'s time, and latterly many of them have been planned with the object of training teachers to run such courses themselves.

It will be seen from this that H.M. Inspectorate alone does quite a considerable job in guiding and supporting teachers, and thus diminishing the possible disadvantage of the

libertarian English system. But a body of only 543, however
excellent its quality, cannot do all that is needed, and many
L.E.A.s maintain a staff of men and women, called variously
inspectors, advisers and organisers, who perform a similar
function though in a somewhat different way. These local
officials, whatever they are called, usually spend a good deal
of their time on administrative matters, but they also visit
schools for educational purposes and organise teachers'
courses. While the Department's short courses are residential
and draw teachers from all over England and Wales and
often from abroad as well, the L.E.A. courses are local and
more often occur in the evenings or at weekends over a
period of weeks or months. They consist, typically, of lectures
and discussions, or of training classes in movement or
music. Only about 50 of the 162 L.E.A.s[25] in England and
Wales maintain a staff of advisers, apart from those concerned
with youth and school meals whose appointment is obligatory,
and, important and valuable as their contribution is, it is
inevitably much less comprehensive than that of H.M.
Inspectorate. The Plowden Council, when they looked into
the matter, concluded that the amount of advice and inspec-
tion available to teachers as a whole was too little rather than
too much.

In 1964 a third organisation, of a very different kind, came
into existence after a year of careful and intensive planning—
the Schools Council for the Curriculum and Examinations.
It is unnecessary to describe here the origins of this body
save to say that they lay in the long-established Secondary
Schools Examination Council and in the new Curriculum
Study Group which had been set up internally in the
Ministry of Education (now D.E.S.) in 1961. The Schools
Council, as now established, is a large body on which the
universities and all major institutions concerned with
education are represented, with an absolute and guaranteed
majority of teachers. This majority is repeated on all the
sub-committees and working parties of the Council, apart
from the one concerned with administration and finance.
The examinations work of the Council does not concern
us here. On the Curriculum side it undertakes projects and

enquiries, following the requests and suggestions of its constituent members, subject to the decisions of its various committees. The way in which each project or enquiry is planned depends upon its nature, but, wherever appropriate, a team is set up consisting of some full-time and some part-time members, all seconded for the purpose and drawn typically from four sources, the universities, H.M. Inspectorate, L.E.A.s and the teaching profession. This kind of partnership is something new in English education. Also new is the opportunity given to practising teachers to take part in enquiries of this kind and that of trying out ideas in schools while the enquiry is in progress. The French project and the mathematics project mentioned in earlier chapters are examples of what has already been done.

While H.M. Inspectorate and the L.E.A.s represent what is fundamentally an authoritarian approach, in that their members have a right of entry into the schools and the power of reporting on teachers' work, the Schools Council provides a machinery for teachers to control their own work. Some have seen in the Council something which will make the two kinds of inspectorate unnecessary and will ultimately replace them. It is always rash to prophesy but this does not seem to me a very likely event. The functions of the Schools Council and of the two inspectorates are quite different, and where they overlap they have led, so far at any rate, to co-operation and not to competition. The Council cannot and could not conceivably cover the ground that the two inspectorates work in, at least without employing a body which was doing much the same work. Already, and long before the Council came into existence, the inspectorates have developed a relationship with the teachers in which the emphasis is on being colleagues rather than important visitors. The most likely development seems to be that the three organisations will grow alongside each other, with increasing co-operation and with perhaps some small redistribution of functions. The in-service training of teachers, for example, which will certainly be needed in addition to courses, may well become the responsibility of the Council, though even here it will be the L.E.A.s which will have to establish the centres in which the training takes place. The L.E.A.s are themselves constituent members of the Council through their associations and H.M.I.s are members or assessors of its committees, so that, although it is a new and very important instrument for improving the schools, it does not look like putting either of the older ones out of business. What is really most significant about it is that it continues, in a new way, the emphasis laid in England on the enterprise and responsibility of the teacher. The outcome of its projects and enquiries, whether they take the form of reports or of teaching material, will not be a programme for all to follow, but something which the individual teacher can use or reject, and, which if he does use it, will still require his initiative and make demands upon his thought. If ever the Council starts producing programmes the danger signal should be hoisted immediately. If it comes on as it has started, parents should welcome it as an instrument of intelligent and tested innovation.[26]

CHAPTER THIRTEEN

Your child and mine

I have tried in this book to describe some of the most interesting things which are going on in the primary schools of today and to explain why they are being done. There are, obviously, a lot of things that I have not mentioned at all and I want, in this final chapter, to refer to two or three of these and then to sum up what I think ought to be the attitude of all of us, parents, general public, ratepayers and taxpayers to primary education.

I have said nothing about teaching machines. Projectors, record-players, radios and television sets, and tape-recorders are all kinds of teaching machines which are used in schools and which all have their uses. They enable teachers to bring into school and to present to the children, material from which they can learn and which they can use for their own purposes. They do not differ essentially from books and pictures, which are the oldest 'teaching machines' of all. However, when people talk about 'teaching machines' they do not really mean all this. They mean machines which give lessons which teach the children some process or set of facts that they would otherwise be taught by the teacher. Two different attitudes to these machines are common. There is the attitude that England is behind the U.S.A. in this kind of thing, that the Americans, being go-ahead, are using teaching machines and that, if we want to be 'with it', we had better hurry up and bring them in. The other attitude is that machines are cold and inhuman, that they cannot have the contact with the children which is the teacher's art and that the whole business is a commercial racket. Neither of these attitudes is very sensible.

The actual teaching machine is simply a mechanical device

for presenting teaching material to the pupils, and in this respect is exactly the same as the projector or T.V. set. The important thing in both cases is the programme. An ordinary arithmetic text-book is a kind of programme. It arranges the material to be learned in a certain order and sets out the steps by which the learning is to be done. The teaching-machine programme does exactly the same but in a much more carefully constructed way. The programmes are of two kinds, linear and branching, each of which has its convinced and even aggressive supporters. The principle of the linear programme is that, whatever is to be learned is divided up into a number of very small steps, each so small that the move forward is very easy, and success is practically assured. The pupil works through this programme on his own and, at the end, the process is complete. The principle of the branching programme is that at each step the pupil is presented with a number of alternatives of which only one is right. If he chooses the right one, i.e. if he understands the point that he is learning, he is taken on to the next step. If he chooses one of the wrong alternatives he is led along a sort of side-road which shows him where he has gone wrong and why and thence back to the main track.

Without going into the merits and demerits of the two systems, linear and branching, it is obvious that this kind of learning has certain great advantages. Provided that each child has a machine and that the programme is well-devised, children can learn at their own pace, they are taught by something which never gets tired or impatient, which is never called away to attend to another child or to speak to the Headmaster and which does not present any personal-relationship problem to him. One of the most successful uses of machines has been in teaching a class of backward junior and secondary children to read.[27] In this instance the novelty of the machine and its impersonalness, against a background of repeated failure with normal methods, undoubtedly contributed to the success of the experiment.

The fact is that we need to know much more about programmed learning than we do at present, before coming to a decision about its place in primary schools. There is some evidence that, after the first excitement of novelty, the children get bored, and some that the learning achieved by linear programmes does not 'stick', that by making each step very easy some necessary element is removed from the process. The D.E.S. has commissioned some research into the matter and this is being undertaken by the University of Sheffield. In the meantime an attitude of sympathetic but vigilant interest seems to be the right one to adopt.

There is one form of mechanical aid which has been in use for many years, the radio, to which, since the war, television has been added. It is impossible to do justice to the work of the School Broadcasting Departments of the B.B.C. and Independent Television Authority within the compass of this book. They provide an immense quantity of material, linguistic, musical, mathematical, biological, geographical, etc., which can be used to supplement, enrich and diversify what is provided in the schools. They make it possible for children to hear new voices and expert performance and to see much that they would otherwise miss. The programmes are prepared with great care and submitted to the continual scrutiny of panels of teachers and inspectors and, in general, a very high standard both of material and of presentation is maintained. The use made of this material depends, like everything else, upon the quality and skill of the teachers in the schools. If the programme is simply switched-on to save trouble, or without preparation and follow-up, the impact on the children is very slight. In periods and in areas of staffing difficulty, where teachers may be constantly changing, school broadcasting and television may provide continuity and quality, but will not turn a poor school into a good one. The best teachers use these services sparingly and selectively, and often record radio programmes on tape for use when required. When video-tape recorders become cheaper and more accessible to amateur use (and this, I understand, is not far off) they will greatly increase the possibilities of television as an educational medium, because it will enable the teachers to integrate what the programmes offer with the hour-to-hour events and needs of the school.

I have made only passing reference to handicapped

children. This was intentional, because the approach and the methods that I have been describing are, I believe, suitable for all children and adaptable to the whole range of intelligence. There are certain handicaps, total deafness and blindness and acute forms of cerebral palsy for example, which need all sorts of additional help, some of which can only be given in schools designed and organised for the purpose. Some other handicaps can be looked after in the ordinary schools, sometimes in special classes as for the partially sighted and sometimes in the ordinary classes. The allowance made for individual variation in need, speed, interest and capacity by the modern primary school, makes it far better adapted to cope with the less able or the difficult child than the traditional school, which relegated the less able to the back of the class and waged continual warfare with the difficult ones. This does not mean to say that the modern approach solves all problems, but it does provide something that is much less of a strait-jacket than the older kinds of school and therefore makes provision for a wider range of child. If a particular child, whether because of maladjustment, or low intelligence, or physical disability is beyond its powers to cope, the school medical service is there to recommend or provide treatment or special provision.

There has lately been a good deal of talk about the 'gifted' child, the child with an exceptionally high intelligence or with unusual powers in music or art. Parents who possess such children may wonder whether the modern primary school makes proper provision for them. Up to a point at least the same thing applies to them as to the handicapped. Modern primary school methods are adaptable to the highly intelligent and, by the scope they offer for individual enterprise and enquiry, are far less likely to frustrate them than was the old formal, rigid teaching. I do not think that anyone who has read this book will dispute this. Whether in fact the highly gifted *do* flourish in ordinary primary schools is, however, another matter. Their needs seem to include contact with others, adults and children, who have the same kind of intelligence as their own and there are schools in which this would not happen. Only 5% of the total population have I.Q.s of 125 or over, and only 0.5 of 140 or over.[28] There are schools and whole areas in which the gifted child might never meet another like him of his own age. Besides, there are some teachers who not only cannot provide the gifted with what they need but think it wrong to do so. They talk about 'equal treatment for all' and confuse it with 'fair treatment for all'. The two would only be the same if we were all identical, and since we are all different 'fair treatment' would ideally mean 'different treatment for all'. The modern primary school does try to give that, to meet, as far as it can, the needs of every individual child and it would be a tragedy if this were ever interfered with by muddle-headed egalitarians.

All parents who bring their children to school when they are 4 or 5 are really saying to the teachers: 'Here is our child whom we have reared and cared for and loved and now we entrust him for part of his day to you, to continue what we have begun and to co-operate with us in helping him to grow fully and healthily and happily'. And every teacher who receives a child is saying to his parents: 'This child of yours is now also in a sense mine, because I have taken on the responsibility of teaching him and I can only do this if I know him and understand him and if you work with me'. Both parents and teachers must say: 'Your child and mine'. If they really do say this and act on it, if the words I have just put into their mouths are really true, the child will have a good chance. To the extent that they are not true that chance is diminished.

If the chance is to be as good as it can be there is someone else who must also say 'Your child and mine'—namely everyone—the voter, the taxpayer, the motorist, the passer-by, you 'hypocrite lecteur, mon semblable, mon frère'.[29] This does not mean being sentimental about children ('dear little things') or foolishly indulgent ('the child is always right') or forcing them into premature and precocious importance, mistakes that many have made in England and elsewhere. It means regarding them as our responsibility and not only that of their parents or teachers, and not only when they are naughty or noisy or ill or distressed—or expensive.

Education costs a lot of money. That is quite unavoidable. There is no such thing as a good, cheap education and anyone who offers you one is a charlatan. Whether it is paid for in fees at an independent school or through rates and taxes at a maintained school it is bound to be expensive. Everyone therefore has a financial interest in it, whether he likes it or not. I hope that for readers of this book that will not be the end of the matter, and that, whether they have children of their own or not, they will feel some responsibility for the nation's schools and some personal concern for the education that is being provided there.

References

1   p. 5   *World Survey of Education Vol. 2, Primary Education UNESCO 1958.*

2   p. 10   *Challenge and Response* Ministry of Education Pamphlet No. 17 HMSO 1950. (An account of the Emergency Scheme for the training of teachers.)

3   p. 12   *Children and their Primary Schools* (Plowden Report) Vol. 1. para. 267–276.

4   p. 12   *Children and their Primary Schools* (Plowden Report) Vol. 1. para. 1081–1085.

5   p. 17   *Children and their Primary Schools* (Plowden Report) Vol. 1. para. 40–41.

6   p. 20   Burt, Cyril. *Mental and Scholastic Tests.* 4th Edn. 1962,p. 145. Staples Press.

7   p. 22   Tanner, J. M. *Education and Physical Growth*, University of London Press 1961, p. 107.

8   p. 23   *Children and their Primary Schools* (Plowden Report) Vol. 2. Appendices 3 and 4 generally esp. para. 2.20 to 2.34 and 4.1 to 4.10.

9   p. 33   Lawrence,D. H. *Pansies*, 2nd Edn., p. 41.

10   p. 53   *Children and their Primary Schools* (Plowden Report) Vol. 1. para. 806–825.

11   p. 59   *Progress in Reading* (Department of Education and Science Education Pamphlet No. 50). HMSO 1966, and Morris, Joyce, *Standards and Progress in Reading.* NFER 1966.

12   p. 59   Downing, John. *The Initial Teaching Alphabet.* Cassell 1966.

13   p. 61   Unpublished survey of ITA by HM Inspectors of Schools.

14   p. 86   Piaget, Jean. *The Child's Conception of Number*.
              Routledge & Kegan Paul 1952.
15   p. 88   Smith, Thyra. *The Story of Numbers*. Part 2,
              'The Discovery of O'. Blackwell 1959.
16   p. 100   Masterman, M. *Theoria to Theory*. Vol. 1, 1966,
              p. 68.
17   p. 107   *Primary Education*. HMSO 1959.
18   p. 107   Schools Council. *French in the Primary School*.
              Field Report No. 2. 1965.
19   p. 131   Education Act of 1944 §25(2).
20   p. 132   *Children and their Primary Schools* (Plowden
              Report) Vol. 1, Chap. 17. See also Survey by
              National Opinion Polls for *New Society* 1965.
21   p. 132   *Children and their Primary Schools* (Plowden
              Report) Vol. 1, pp. 489–493.
22   p. 132   Goldman, R. J. *Religious Thinking from Childhood
              to Adolescence* (esp. pp. 220–234). Routledge
              & Kegan Paul 1964.
23   p. 133   Education Act of 1944 §25(1).
24   p. 135   Education Act of 1944 §26.
25   p. 136   *Children and their Primary Schools* (Plowden
              Report) Vol. 1, para. 947.
26   p. 140   Department of Education and Science. *Reports
              on Education* No. 29. HMSO 1966, and
              Challenge and Response HMSO 1966.
27   p. 142   Evidence submitted to Plowden Council 1965.
28   p. 145   *Children and their Primary Schools* (Plowden
              Report) Vol. 1, para. 862.
29   p. 145   Baudelaire. *Les Fleurs du Mal*.

*Children and their Primary Schools—A report of the Central
Advisory Council for Education (England)* is published by
HMSO and is in two volumes.